Change

How to Become
The Woman He Wants

Kenya K. Stevens

Self-As-Source® Publishers, Atlanta

First Edition

ISBN: 978-0-9801663-3-0
              0-9801663-3-0

Published By: Self-As-Source Publishing LLC

Web Address: www.selfassource.com

Cover Image: Keston Duke, Keston Duke Photography
www.kestonduke.com

Cover Design: Dunn+Associates

Edited By: Aneesah Akram – www.speedyfingertips.com
(Coming soon)

Email: speedyfingertips@comcast.net

Formatting By: Rakhem Seku

To find out more about the author check out:
www.jujumama.com | www.sunrazecoaching.com

For my husband,
Carl E. Stevens Jr. | Rakhem Seku,
who taught me that a little respect goes a long way in receiving the love I
desire. I will always love you and give you my very best self. You are my
mirror – my reflection looks darn good right about now!

To Ancient Women of all races,
I thank you for aiding me on my journey into womanhood. I know that
you have been there for me, watching, whispering; and supporting me all
along the way...

♀ Change Your Man ♂

Table of Contents

Introduction

OK, I have a confession to make. For many years, I behaved very badly in my marriage. I was controlling, spoiled, immature, needy, and even violent. Not only did I behave badly, but also I have come to realize that deep inside I was afraid to let go of my disruptive, disagreeable behaviors. I felt as though I had access to power only through the forceful behaviors that felt natural for me. I did not want to accept my role as nurturer, mother, and wife. The traditional, domestic female archetypes seemed weak and powerless. I did not want to be vulnerable or sweet to my husband for fear that he would take advantage of me. I preferred the strong, willful, and direct approach. Seizing each opportunity to proclaim sovereignty and control, I unwittingly became the 'man' of the house.

Yet at the same time, I wanted to be treated like an absolute queen. Wine me, dine me, adore my beauty, make love to me and worship at the shrine of my depleted feminine essence. What a quandary. I wanted desperately to be the man and the woman in my relationship. Being the woman was acceptable for most holidays such as Valentine's Day, birthdays, anniversaries and especially Mother's Day, which he had better not ever forget. But other than that, treat me as the boss, the big man! Our home was a war zone until the day I realized the issue, I was failing at marriage and the cause was ME. I could not blame my husband for my misery any longer.

Changing for the better essentially changed my man, and as chance would have it, it happened by accident. I developed a serious life-threatening illness, and for the first time in our marriage, I became vulnerable to my husband in the blink of an eye. As this life-altering health challenge intensified, I began to realize the error in my ways. I realized that I did not appreciate or trust my husband, nor was I being the type of wife who elicited his love. The answer to the truth about my own actions, attitudes and beliefs was something that spoke personally to me from deep within. I had to begin to tell myself the truth and stop the incessant blaming and complaining about my husband. As I began to discover and admit to my own folly, an incredible internal journey began.

What is the importance of standing naked in truth? Well the old folks say, "The truth shall set you free." Telling the truth about my relationship is the most freeing act that I ever initiated at my own expense. Once I decided to take responsibility for my behaviors knowing that I am creating my life with my thoughts and actions, the entire Universe shifted to help me to heal. I began to discover books. The first was The Proper Care and Feeding of Husbands by Dr. Laura Schlesinger. I read each of her books and then moved on to The Surrendered Wife series by Laura Doyle.

I further enhanced my understanding by thoroughly studying John Grey's piece, Men Are from Mars, Women Are from Venus. Collectively, the combination of my own inner truth and revelations and this new information about how men are affected by women's moods and actions began to grow me way beyond my old, stubborn shell. Reluctantly, I slowly began to make small changes, and as I did, my husband began to change magically. As I progressed in accepting and integrating new information about the power of femininity, I single handedly saved my marriage and my life, and I became free of the illness in no time.

I strongly believe the importance of my ordeal is so that others can benefit from my story. I truly have learned the secrets to changing my man. I used to hear women say that it is impossible to change a man. I beg to differ! I have seen the changes in my man since I changed my own irrational fear of losing control. I have seen my husband become willing to please me as I became more appreciative of each little thing he did. I have witnessed him rise to protect and take care of me as I began to trust him unconditionally.

It is all about the power of being a woman. You know who you are; you are just like me. You are good looking and smart, confident and sophisticated, independent and strong. You might have a great job and maybe many college degrees. You put on your tough, masculine shell in order to burst the glass ceiling to survive the degradation of having to be perfect and remain sane in a society that expects you to be androgynous. When deep inside, you have buried your feminine nature only to drudge her up strategically to win favor in life. You hide from your natural feminine qualities to protect yourself from being eaten alive in this seemingly male dominated culture, and rightfully so. So when you do find love, most of the time it dwindles when you realize that he is not going to serve your every need or fulfill your every desire. To be vulnerable, open, and feminine with the opposite sex is not the norm, so it is a challenge to learn and practice the art of true womanhood.

In order to change my man, I had to rekindle my role as the woman. I had to submit (curse word, I know). If this word feels like a curse word to you, then you really need to read this book. Indeed, I had to submit to my real inner powers to change my life and my man. Submitting to my husband came later and not without long days and nights – years even – of misunderstandings and hardships. Reading about my transformation may seem challenging at first, but I weave into the chapters proof that restoring sane womanhood is easier than it sounds and that it has many rewards.

I share my personal journey in marriage so that you can peek into the ways that I changed my man by losing the diva image. Alas, the control freak in me awakened to her femininity and achieved the true power to create all that I desire. I share with you nine very spiritual processes that came to me when I asked the Universe to show me how to change, and also the nine principles that changed my man for good. I believe that you will love knowing how these principles and processes altered the course of my life and even healed me from a life-threatening reproductive illness. Knowing my step-by-step processes will arm you with substantial information on how to change your man and heal your relationship.

Part One – *Stop Confronting Him*, is about how direct confrontation of a man pushes him deep into a cave with no access to even the woman he loves. Passive-aggressive confrontations, as well as outward-aggressive behaviors, have devastating effects on our love lives. I provide healing processes that can be done in 15 minutes or less to help women shift these troubled spots. In Part Two – *Stop Directing Him*, I will explain how giving directions to a man can shut him away from you on the deepest levels. You will discover the smooth, sexy art of making your relationship work, and getting exactly what you want from your man without giving direct orders.

By now, many of you might be asking yourselves some very important questions. Can I really change my man? Do I feel comfortable being a woman? Is my denial of true womanhood wreaking havoc in my relationship? I invite you to take the following survey to assess this for yourself. Be honest with yourself and answer each question yes or no.

Change Your Man Pop Quiz

1. Do you get upset when the man in your life will not do what you feel he should do? Yes or No
2. Do you tell him what to do or how to behave? Yes or No
3. Is he always wrong, misinformed or ignorant about simple things? Yes or No

4.   Does he shirk responsibilities at home while you take up the slack? Yes or No
5.   Do you feel as though he avoids talking to you by choosing TV, work, or any other distraction over conversation with you? Yes or No

If you answered yes to even one of these questions, this book is definitely for you. It is time for you to change your situation and change your man. You will do this with ease as you change your own behaviors. For once, it is not relevant to place blame. You will not heal your current or future relationships by blaming him or yourself, life in general, or by breaking up with him. You will just invent another man who will push you to take a similar journey into your own womanhood. The work that we will do together is about understanding how to live a different life. I want you to have it easy like me. Change your man and reclaim yourself as a woman. Take a spiritual journey with me as we incorporate the Law of Attraction and other Universal Principles in a process that will be just as easy as it fun.

Benefits of Reading Change Your Man

- Rekindle the love and intimacy in your marriage.
- Feel happy and successful as a woman.
- Teach your daughters how to be feminine and relaxed through your example.
- Learn the 12 secrets to rekindling your femininity.
- Discover 12 fun and easy processes to increase your femininity.
- Become the type of woman that every man loves.
- Improve your relationship with your father, boss, brothers and all men.
- Improve your relationships with women.
- Feel peaceful and relaxed every day.
- Enjoy your life as a woman by maintaining feelings of bliss all the time.

The Four Elements of Femininity

Since writing Book One: *Change Your Man*, my husband and I have been traveling the country speaking about the laws outlined in this book. We have since developed the eight attributes of masculinity and femininity; four archetypes for women, and four for men. I want to briefly explain these laws, as they will assist you as you read this book. Keep in mind that each law is expandable and can be form fit to your personality.

The relationship between male and female energy is simple to summarize when looked at through the lens of the attributes below:

Female Trait Visionary	Male Trait Monk

The **Visionary** is the first female attribute. She trusts her man. The trust that she has for her man is unconditional. Her optimism and faith in him is not based upon what he has done in the past, nor is it based upon how men have treated her in the past... but is based on what she knows she deserves. Her thought about what he *can and will* do is optimistic. She has a vision of goodness for her life and her man naturally fits the vision. This blind faith is the power that actually *creates*, in her man, the ability to accomplish any task. This is not something that mother has taught us in this day and age.

Thus, this **Visionary** trait must be cultivated. Using the principles and exercises in this book will aid women in cultivating the *Visionary* within.

Once a woman is in a **Visionary** mode, her man will assume the posture of **Monk**. The **Monk** is a planner; he will always take the lead in creating plans for the family, long and short term. Most men aspire to be in the **Monk** position, setting goals and objectives for the family and receiving his mate's buy-in. Often men do not find their mates so cooperative and trusting of his plans and thus, quits. It takes a strong **Visionary** woman to create a man who is confident enough to use his intuition to set short and long term objectives for his family. A woman who is not a **Visionary** will debate with his plans or demonstrate lack of faith in his ability to plan, thus making it impossible for him to play his position. In the long run, when women do not have faith in a man to plan for his family, she will end up taking the position of **Monk** because he will not "step up".

I speak more about the **Visionary** position in chapters One and Six.

Female Trait Devotee	Male Trait Leader

The next female trait is what we call the **Devotee**. This woman is devoted to her man will always be willing to follow his lead. He becomes her manager. When the **Devotee** demonstrates her ability to follow his guidance, he becomes a powerful **Leader**. The **Devotee** is surrendered, submissive, nurturing, and powerfully endowed with the ability to motivate her man's actions using the power of meditation and trance.

Here is what I mean. A **Devotee** is perfectly willing to use her *Psychic Womb* instead of external means to accomplish her objectives. The *Psychic Womb* is something that all women have access to. This is the part of a woman, though unseen comprises her most massive ability to effect change in the world and in her relationship. In a word, the *Psychic Womb* is her temple; to expand that definition, the Psychic Womb is much like the physical womb in that it can bring reality into existence. Just as a woman can birth a baby, she can also birth any 'reality' onto the planet. Men know this, and look for women who have strong psychic influence. If you have ever heard the phrase "behind every great man is a powerful woman" this encapsulates what is meant by the role of **Devotee**.

The **Devotee** makes her man strong and powerful by refraining from confronting him, which we dive into extensively in this book. Her **Leader** is her darling spouse, and thus, she recognizes him as such. Does this mean she has no power? No. Women have vastly different power than men; men are externally focused while men are internally focused. In other words, a **Devotee** realizes that she does not have to use physical means of communication and/or force to magnetize his honorable leadership and duty to the family. Instead, she simply becomes aware of what she desires of him and visualizes that desire into her *Psychic Womb*. There, she creates a vision of her man doing what she needs him to do and it begins to occur in reality.

She is never bossy, dictatorial, dismissive or overbearing. She knows that she holds the power in her family not because she is forceful and verbose, but because she has the power to create anything with her *Psychic Womb*. Thus, she follows when her man leads the external areas of her life. And she runs the show internally by simply visualizing what she desires.

Men who have strong **Devotee's** for wives find themselves empowered to be accountable, managerial and strong minded. She accepts him as her leader and thus goes to him for advice. When he needs advice from her, he asks her. She does not immediately give it, but meditates on the concern and brings him information from the inner world. She is profoundly connected to Source. When she uses her power to meditate and hear Source Energy within herself, and brings information from meditation directly to him, he finds himself in service to her. His service is made easy by her surrendered disposition and strong emotional support.

An added benefit to both man and woman in this situation is that the woman becomes the Receiver and the man becomes the Giver. What is meant is that the Devotee is primarily a receiver. She receives instructions from her man, and agrees to follow, as well; she receives instructions from Source (some call this God, Jesus, Buddha, Jehovah…) and is able to convey these messages with clarity to her man. The reason this is important is because men are born on this planet already knowing how to receive… men are on Earth learning to give, serve and protect. Women are born knowing innately how to give; we are here on this Planet learning how to receive. To become a receptive and nurturing Devotee is critical.

More can be found on the **Devotee** in chapters… Two, Eight and Ten.

Female Trait Conservationist	Male Trait Soldier

The next feminine trait of the four is the **Conservationist.** The **Conservationist** is extremely self-focused. She is most concerned about her own welfare and secondly about that of her family and husband/mate. She is focused on herself because she knows that she has to be at her highest energy level in order to be whom she must for her family and household. If she is not feeling well, the entire family is in jeopardy. In other words, if the woman of the home is ill, tired, overworked, or ignoring her own personal needs, she will not be able to function at her best in her family. So she conserves her energy.

The **Conservationist** is so keenly focused on her own well being that she never takes on more chores, work, or play than she can handle. If her chores are a bit much, she goes to her mate for advice about how to handle the stress. She takes his advice and implements new ways of being, anything to make her life easier.

When she is taking care of herself, she produces a male who is a **Soldier**. This male type is keenly interested in securing her, providing for her and making her life and the life of the family easier. He concerns himself with sacrificing all that is needed to create an environment for her that she can further relax into. He loves that she is stress free and relaxed and his only duty becomes to make her even more comfortable.

When a woman chooses to be a **Conservationist**, she has time to take her remedies, oil her body, enjoy a bath, and follow her dreams and hobbies. She becomes an asset to the family because she also has extra energy left over to serve her family providing remedies, foods, and cleanliness in her household. She is also good with conserving resources, measuring each amount of time, money or energy carefully so that too much is never extended. She is contracting as her man expands. She is living a peaceful life of ease making it possible for her man to take on more in the external world to secure her.

The **Conservationist** is healthy, relaxed, self-focused and wise. She is also organized, neat, and clean and understands what is needed to harmonize her own energy and that of her family and household. Again, and most importantly, she never bites off more than she can chew.

More can be found on the Conservationist in chapter Four.

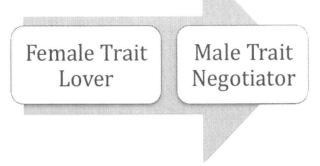

Female Trait
Lover

Male Trait
Negotiator

The final feminine trait for women is the **Lover**. The **Lover** is most certainly beautiful, inside and out. Most importantly, she is pleasable. She is able to smile, relax and appreciate her man sexually, and otherwise. She is actually a magnet for love.

Her luscious, fresh demeanor endears her man to her. She is willing at all times to be pleased by him.

When the **Lover** is strong in a woman, she produces a man who is a **Negotiator**. This is the type of man who has excellent communication skills and blatant ability to route funds and other needed resources to the house. He becomes all the more skillful at working out resource issues in the larger world because she is so pleased by him, and complimentary and appreciative of his efforts. He is so powerful because he naturally pleases her. Everything that he does well, she acknowledges. And as for the things that he is not so good at, she is never complaining about them, but using her **Devotee** strength to visualize the best.

The **Lover** speaks well of her husband/mate in public and in private. She is always willing to see that he is doing his best, and thus, he will always be inclined to do better. She knows the secrets of sensual interaction. She is willing to receive in the bedroom, rather than putting on a show, or giving too much. I will explain this in later chapters.

She follows his lead and is always receptive to his advances. She teaches him how to love her using her sounds, body and reactions to him. She never gives him full out verbal instructions. When she likes what he is doing sensually, she reacts with her energy... when she does not like it, she is still willing to relax into it and wait for the goodness to flow, which is always her expectation... for goodness to flow.

Her words are few, but pleasant. She is less into verbal language and more into body language and the languages of the soul. As her language softens and becomes energy based, his language hardens and becomes verbally more demonstrative. Daily he becomes more capable of communication because he is forced to fill the vacuum of her sweet silence and receptive smile. So blissful! Ummm.....

♀ Change Your Man ♂

More can be found on the Lover in Chapters three, five, and seven.

PART ONE: Make Him into a Man

Stop Confronting Him

In the beginning of my marriage, I had no idea what the problem was. Why the constant turbulence? What were all the arguments really about? Today, I cannot remember the specific causes of each blow up. I do, however, have sour memories of lamps being thrown, threats to break up, chasing him outdoors at night, yelling at one another, throwing my wedding ring at him, crying all night and even some physical violence usually initiated by me…I secretly loved provoking him into emotional drama. He so often ignored my needs and desires that it seemed as though it was only when he was provoked that I would see in him the passion that I craved. I wanted him to man up and take responsibility for me. I needed him to care about my feelings and feel the need to protect and cherish me. These early confrontations were the most brutal, but they still did not help me get what I wanted. I thought I could change my man into that adoring, loving person I needed by confronting him.

I recall directly confronting my husband about things that I wanted him to change like his attitude, priorities and habits. Much of our relationship energy focused on the various issues I had with him. I could find fault with him as quickly as a baby finds something to put in its mouth. When I found something to gripe about, I did it complaining without realizing how badly it was truly affecting our marriage. I managed it so subtly that I probably would not have called it nagging back then. I would have defended my right to discuss my opinions; I had the right to communicate when 'issues' surfaced, right? Don't you feel this way, ladies? We call it 'being honest'. My logic was that by focusing on his issues I was asserting myself by asking for and getting what I wanted in my relationship. All he had to do was to accept what I was saying and change his behavior.

Had I known at that time, based on the Law of Attraction, which simply states 'what you focus on expands', that focusing on his issues would expand his issues, I might have begun shifting away from having to talk all night about bullshit that happened days ago. If at that time I had a full understanding of the Law of Attraction, which also states, "That which is like unto itself is drawn," I may have opened to releasing the need to complain and blame. I had no idea that by confronting the problems I saw in him, I became a huge part of the problem. Being a part of the solution would have been a better option. I was killing all potential of having the happiness I desired by finding fault, confronting, and blaming him for all of our troubles.

In any given week, I might complain ten times as much as I showed Carl any form of appreciation or affection. It was very unusual for me to give him simple praise. I cannot recall giving him as many compliments as I did complaints. Compliments and praise for my husband just went underemphasized. Instead, the norm in our communication was a constant flow of little comments about things that he should have done, did not do, or needed to do better. I had a nice tone of voice, so I did not yell at him. I just pointed out the negative and the mistakes I felt he was making. I had no idea how unevenly the compliments and critiques were distributed; the critiques seemed more relevant, of course, while I reserved the compliments for special moments when he was really shining brightly. Even then, it was hard to open my mouth and express my gratitude.

There was rarely a day that I simply honored him and respected him for who he was. I almost never thanked him for being my husband and my very best friend. My husband has always been a kind and gentle man. He is an upstanding guy with lots of positive traits. Sure, he has some of the typical habits and faults that other men have, but my goodness, I have just as many quirks as he does. Why was I not able to express my delight as easily as I expressed displeasure? I do not allow myself the lame excuse that I had forgotten what it was that attracted me to him in the first place. I knew very well what I loved about my sexy, strong and intelligent husband who had stood by me each day of our marriage. It was easy to think of these things in my mind, but sharing them came only after endless direct confrontations and negative badgering. When we reconciled after an argument I would sneak some affection and appreciation into the mix.

When I really think back to those painful years, I guess that I do recall the butt of the issues. Mostly, I did not want him to do things that irritated me. The list of irritating things included all the actions that negated my opinions and expectations of him. I wanted him to fit into my world nicely like a new piece of furniture. You turn it this way and push it around, you find the perfect place for it and there it stays nice and neat, good to look at and heaven to sit on. Until, of course, spring comes and the room is redecorated with all new colors and a nice new cover for the furniture. I learned the hard way that a man is not a piece of furniture, you cannot shift him into a more suitable behavior, and you will definitely not change his personality to suit your moods by openly confronting him.

In this chapter, I will give you my definition of direct confrontations and share stories that will invite you to live vicariously through my marriage to experience the sting of these wars of words. Confronting a man is the metaphorical equivalent of shifting a couch to suit your mood. There are so many womanly options besides simply getting in his face. We have to learn to use the power within in a more subtle way to affect reality. We do have the power to change our men. The truth is that many women have not recognized this pattern of behavior so direct confrontations are usually done by accident. Let's define direct confrontation and then look at origins of this behavior and apply easy, subtle solutions to the problem.

Direct Confrontation Defined

When I use the term direct confrontation, I am speaking of a situation in which a woman in a relationship finds herself engaging her mate with exaggerated emotion regarding a matter of her own opinion. She engages her mate in an attempt to be right in the situation, therefore directly confronting him to elicit an instantaneous move or action on his part towards acceptance of her view and compliance to her rules. It is direct because she is using language and tone that reflects her belief that she is right.

Please do not confuse a direct confrontation with a wish to communicate or to compromise on an issue. Compromise is something altogether different, and it does not begin with a confrontation, it begins with love. A woman from a place of love becomes vulnerable instead of angry and asks for a meeting with her beloved. A meeting happens, preferably at the man's initiation, where the main agenda item is love, praise, appreciation and resolution to an issue or concern. There is no attack, accusation, attitude, or disrespectful language.

When a direct confrontation occurs, there is little or no original desire to compromise on the part of the woman. In fact, most often the objective on the part of the female is to dominate the situation and be correct about it. I know from my own experience that when I confronted my mate about taking the garbage out, working with the children or spending more quality time with me, I wanted to have things go my way. It took a moment to wake up to this reality. Nonetheless, it was indeed fact that I confronted my mate, even if politely, to gain accesses to having things go my way.

Another key point to note about direct confrontation is that there is usually not a conflict at hand. Most often, things are going well and seemingly calm, when out-of-the-blue comes a request. The male of the house may be thinking, working or focused on something else when the woman begins bringing new complaints, requests, and/or demands to the table. The stance that most males take when these confrontations occur is one of surprise and then defense, thus the birth of conflict.

Why Do We Confront our Men?

In my marriage, I subconsciously initiated these direct confrontations almost daily. Eventually, I began to question myself as to why I kept going here with my man. Why was I using such a cold and disrespectful tone of voice? Why was I whining and so emotional about things? Why did I have such an incessant need to be right? Was I born rolling my neck and cutting my eyes? Did I emerge from the womb with the need to give the silent treatment to whomever refuses to comply with my wishes, or was I born predisposed to having to have my way all of the time? If I was born this way, why did my parents not teach me to become an adult and communicate in ways that did not cause such turbulence? Why was I unwilling and unable to compromise, love deeply, unconditionally, and be agreeable in relationships with people? The issues I took with my man did not match the magnitude of my disgust.

Of course, for years it was easy to blame him. After all, everything was entirely his fault. He was the one who always had to obey his ego and pride. He never shared his feelings with me and he always became moody without telling me what I was doing wrong. As far as I was concerned, he was an egotistical, low life and tried to boss me around just because he wanted to be in charge. I hated that all of my requests – simple requests – were greeted with such contempt.

Just basic maintenance of our home became a war zone with the battles fought in our bedroom, yard and kitchen. The towels my man left hanging on the hamper or closet door would set me off, his coming home late from work enraged me, and his forgetting about appointments and dates that we would plan together eroded my trust in him. I became a walking time bomb filled with inner rage. The grass growing taller than our neighbor's and the bushes needing a trim, even after I would ask him nicely to please get it done, became a signal to get ready for war. Little B-52's were the oven needing to be cleaned, and the shoes left near the front door. I could not get out of the war because the bombs kept going off! It was always my thought that I had to retaliate with words. I thought they were nice words for a war... but apparently, words fan the flames of war. Soon our bedroom was full of gunshot holes leaking all the intimacy that I missed. I blamed him because he was the one waging war, or so it seemed, by not doing and being the kind of man that I wanted – neat, efficient, and on top of things. I was trying to keep the peace by allowing him a chance to do things my way. So why was this not working for me? Does it work for you? It must work for someone!

I had to find out where his bad attitude was coming from and why he refused to see that what I wanted him to do was to follow my lead. I thought I should look at him more closely, pick his childhood apart and examine his relationship to his mother. I thought it my duty to fix him with self-help books and counseling. I lectured him for hours at a time trying to find out why he could not do simple things and trying to explain how simple these simple things were. After none of this badgering worked, I realized I had to find a new way. Directly confronting him was not winning me any cool points.

I guess I began to use the same lectures and psychoanalysis on myself that I had used on him in order to find some answers. I began to look deeply into my own consciousness to find the roots, and quickly began to see the origin of my behavior. My confrontational communication style, like yours I bet, began during my early educational experiences. It served me through elementary, middle, high school and then college. In looking back at these areas of my life, I found that the male energy in me was first cultivated, among other things, by the modern educational experience.

Where the Confrontational Gene Began

I know now that I went into marriage ill prepared, as most of us do. It seems the modern educational system spends more time educating us in the ABC's and 123's of linear thinking than anything else. A way to educate kids about emotional issues, or metaphysical thought and relationships has yet to be incorporated into our educational system. Very little time goes to helping us understand how to conduct ourselves properly in relation to others. We did not receive marriage training, just insufficient sex education. My training around marriage as a young girl was in essence, "Don't get into trouble," "Wait until you are married," and "Be independent, don't ever depend on a man to take care of you." On the other hand, the public schools I attended taught me a very intense, male or left-brained thinking approach to life, which proved to be devastating.

The first concept I learned in elementary school is that right and wrong is a concrete, and the second was that we have no choice in how life unfolds and that reality is out there happening to us. Both of these concepts are based on what I have termed a male domination model – conquer, conquest, and separation. Excelling in modern public schools means accepting a male's view of life. This pseudo male energy began for me very early on as I adopted the ways that would get me the straight A's. How about you?

The tests given in the public schools I attended had only one right answer for each problem, all other answers were wrong. Do you remember the big red X? The awful mark that shouted without words – WRONG, STUPID, as though stupid is such a thing. I wanted the golden star so I learned to hate being wrong. Whoever heard of a teacher who encouraged students to make a bad choice, do the problem wrong, try new ways of doing things that will get new answers, or better yet, find your own answers? Not ever did I have a teacher with a more open and integrative style. My teachers taught me that it was good and honorable to get the answers right, so I wanted to be right and learned that being right, at all costs, was important as early as elementary school.

Adhering to a strict value system dictating right and wrong or answering questions correctly awarded passing grades. Our modern educational system also taught us to exclude things that do not belong. Who can forget the puzzles with four items pictured in four separate squares? The directions were to cross out (obliterate) the one that did not belong, and oh my goodness, do not be the one in class who cannot figure this out. Do not be the odd ball. Being right was life or death in the top-notch suburban classrooms I grew up in. No one wanted to be the laughing stock of the school. Singling out the thing that did not belong taught me to look for differences in human beings and then judge others based on these differences. No wonder I found myself in relation to the man of my life focusing on finding the problems. In our relationship, I was still seeking the A's that I had so craved in elementary school when our major tasks included finding the

28

problems and obliterating all that did not fit neatly into our world.

The effect of these common kindergarten exercises, which taught principles of exclusion of difference, concrete right and wrong, and other linear processing on my ability to be a feminine woman was profound. I began to define reality based on a set of unspoken codes of non-acceptance, exaggerated independence, and blatant rejection of the abstract. Essentially, school encouraged the masculine left-brain approach or 'segregate' thinking. Femininity, on the other hand, is right brain oriented – an intuitive, integrative model.

I know that most women today do not like to be classified as intuitive or emotional, but the way that I have experienced my own feminine energy is just that. Nowhere in school, not even in art or home economics, could I develop my natural proclivity for being abstract, intuitive and still 'feel' smart. They even found ways to test us in art classes. To include the concept of right and wrong even in an art class is a telltale sign that the masculine energy in this culture is way out of control. There should be no tests in art! Individuals should be allowed to sense form and experiment with emotion. No experimenting allowed in home economics either. Follow the recipe, make the dish correctly and get an A. How interesting. No wonder so many women are not fond of cooking. All the SOUL was taken out of it when we learned to become male in the kitchen during high school home economics. Even the concept of a bake off is centered in male domination and competition. There is nothing wrong with this, except that we are teaching women to be men by setting our learning systems up through the left-brain worldview.

School taught me that there is one uniformed worldview and I must always conform to it in order to pass muster. School also taught me that I had to be right in order to be considered good, and get passing grades to not be laughed at by friends and family. I carried this ceaseless need to be right into my relationship with my husband; most of us do. This male linear or left-brained approach was the hallmark of all of our educational experiences unless we were educated in alternative environments.

Because school taught me an obsession to being right, I could not afford to be intuitive. The abstract was not something that I had time to think about, since it did not, nor did the metaphysical, spiritual and emotional principles of femininity, have a place in that kind of system. These types of emotions were out of order and were to be ignored. It took too much away from my focus to actually give in to an emotion, ponder an abstract notion or test principles of metaphysical wonderings. WAKE UP and stop daydreaming is what I seemed to hear my teachers exclaim. I was being trained to think like a man from age five. How could I have been expected to welcome my own womanhood when schools taught only the importance of manhood? No wonder our relationships are so imbalanced.

Middle school was no better. I learned that there were stupid people and there were smart people. The stupid people were the ones that sort of fell into the class clown category or the 'bad kid' section. These students did not get the work done correctly or on time (everything was time sensitive, you know). They rebelled against having to put correct answers onto the clean white paper in order to be considered a good person. Instead they sat in the back of the class throwing spitballs (very intuitive and creative), and seemed to have little hope for the future, no place in the classroom, and no respect for the unspoken order. They rebelled against the male structure by doing intuitive things such as singing, making creative jokes, and sleeping.

Those of us who had perfected the art of being right perceived them dumb. These rebellious kids had the wrong answer so many times that it became funny to us. They accepted being the butt of our jokes and even made art of the situation wearing artistic clothing, painting graffiti and doing wild and outrageous stunts to gain acceptance and attention. Somehow, these kids were the cool ones once we reached high school. They had succeeded at bringing the feminine energy into the classrooms to thwart imbalanced male principles. That was nice…but I would not have any part in it.

Neither class clowns nor stupid kids appealed to me. I wanted to be the one on track to make money and make something of myself. The kids on my path who did not buck the system, but rather set out to master it, had to get the answers correct. We had to show up with pointed focus and an air of competition. I was on that path for sure and my parents, grandparents, cousins, neighbors and siblings made sure that I knew I was college bound. They thought it a favor to remind me of how smart I was, and how one day I would be something great like a lawyer or a classical musician.

Even in music class, the masculine thought patterns were present. I always wanted to hear the music and learn to play it based on the sounds I heard, even improvise as a jazz player might. However, I soon learned that to pass the class, I had to conform to the notes on the page. I had to learn the rules, and theory of musical dictation. This was not easy for me, and I got into lots of trouble improvising until I finally submitted to the left-brain and learned to read the notes without any difficulty.

Due to my early training, it was not surprising that I grew into womanhood with an overwhelming and relentless need to be right in every disagreement or circumstance with my man. I was not to be classified as a clown or dummy! I sat in the front of the class where we learned to prove our points and stand in our views of right and wrong. These views, of course, had to be in good standing with the worldview taught in the modern classroom. A smart person, I had to use the masculine, disciplined, structured, ordered, and cerebral side to master school. Many people believe that women do better in school because we are more disciplined than men are, when in fact this is not true; we are more willing to follow than men and therefore can fit the mold we are being poured into. Men rebel, even against a culture that suits their dominant and competitive proclivities because they want to be the makers of the mold; following is not their strong suit. All the same, I morphed into the left side of my brain developing it to the exclusion of the places where feelings, emotions, intuition and acceptance reside. But high school was far worse...

The modern, high-tech high school I attended taught me that our opinions, attitudes and ideas should be the very substance of our lives. I was encouraged to find my voice and refine my views. To most, it might seem liberating that our lives are shaped around our opinions and beliefs. What fun! We can live freely based solely on what seems righteous and logical. We can prove any point we desire to prove as long as we can document the logical line of thought that leads us to form our conclusion. I do not have a problem with this, but how could I truly have an opinion after attending elementary school wherein I was essentially brainwashed into using the left-brain as the source of all reason and rightness? I had already been force fed a linear worldview, and my opinions were molded to uphold the status quo. High school is set up to give a sense of freedom to a group already enslaved into a certain left-brained way of processing reality. This is where I learned to refine this male view of the world. I learned that the next level of education would teach me to refine what I thought was my view and to debate it with others.

In high school, I learned to find the holes in the opinions of others. I learned to directly confront these adverse views in the form of a thesis paper. I learned to structure my point of view in such a manner as to set all other points of view to rest.

My writing courses guided me in the art of defending my views at all costs using the best words in the English language with the aim of proving all other perspectives unfit and unfounded. Girls were the best writers in my class; very seldom were the boys able to debate with such emotion.

I was involved in the debate club, as well as Model United Nations, where I learned to form flawless arguments, find supporters to back my opinion, and to crush all other opinions that seemed to oppose my logical conclusions. I mastered this form of direct confrontation with ease. Divergent viewpoints did not have a chance with me. I learned to prove logically that the sky was green, that night was day and that money did not exist. This was a necessary initiation in preparation for university. By the end of high school I was well on my way to becoming the man that modern education was training me to be. Not only did I debate in class, but also my parents did not stand a chance against my mouth. People pegged me as smart, independent, and already successful. Sure, I had my private moments when I cried and felt lost and lonely, and separated from my authentic self, but to the world, I was going places fast!

I was able to fight my way through and put the masculine icing on the cake in college. I knew how to fake and kiss up to the professors using my beauty (the only part of my feminine essence that was allowed in public). I had learned this tactic well, having been told by educated people that I should do whatever it takes to make the grade - neglect my health, cheat or steal; whatever was required to finish. I was to be a man and compete–be a woman and flirt–be strong or be an airhead, be whatever you have to be to win the race and acquire the diploma. I had truly mastered ignoring my intuitions and my higher conscious. I had to be right at all costs forgiving no one and taking no prisoners – ever. I trusted no one except myself and I made it on my own; I did not need any man, or woman for that matter, to help me. All I needed was a sense of security in the fact that I could out think the world. I was a success at it, and that is all that mattered.

For the 20 years of my educational experience, I had no idea that this was a process of socialization that would make relationships, companionship and even sex more difficult in 50 percent of America – impossible. Yes, the current divorce rate is a stat that supports my idea that our modern cultural paradigm is in need of some serious work. People, in general, are intrinsically ill prepared to have deep, intimate and loving relationships, and women, more specifically, due to having learned to be men in school. Men are ill prepared from having learned to rebel against force-fed masculine thought in school. The divorce rate in the United States is a direct result of the fact that two well-bred men, one a man in woman's clothing and the other an authentic, yet rebellious, mentally castrated man, were never truly meant to co habituate. You know the old sayings 'too many chiefs, no Indians;' 'too much fire and no water.'

This fiery educational training (among other social, economic, psychological factors, of course) landed me knee deep in endless confrontations with my mate. It is truly quite simple. In relationships, there is a great deal of compromise involved. When two wild male forces come to an impasse, there is rarely room for compromise; you can expect a locked-horn fight to the death. And so went my relationships. In school, I learned to battle for the victory of my own perspectives and to fight dirty. I learned that someone had to lose so that I could be the winner. So here it began the unwinding of any possibility for a loving relationship. Yet off I went into the world – the well educated she-man that I was – to find Mr. Right! On top of all of that, I was fearful of losing my sense of freedom and independence. I reveled in the fact that I could make my own decisions, make my own way in the world and do it my way. Boy, Mr. Right was going to have to do a hell of a job to convince me that I should give my perfect self to him. The search was on!

Stumbling Upon My Lost Inner Woman

My relationships in high school were bunked. Because of my linear thinking and having had no introduction to real intimacy between a man and woman, I figured that sex was the real intimacy. All I did in high school was have sex with boys who truly could not care less about me. Of course, I thought they cared, but being detached from my feelings and emotions, I rationalized that this was the way things were. I thought it appropriate to give myself to boys with an expectation that they follow my dictates in return. Walk me to my classes, take me to the prom, and call me every day, and stay on the phone with me all night, blah, blah, blah. It was very robotic. Deep inside I was hurt, alone and afraid, but on the surface I just moved quickly to the next one when the current boy fell away from me. I wanted to meet my man in high school and get married, which would have been the perfect love affair like my parents and grandparents. When it did not happen, I just figured I would wait until college.

College was more of the same. However, I was able to begin to explore new information about life and love. I expanded my view of life while keeping a tight focus on finding Mr. Right and healing myself from this fear, control, and left-brained paradigm. By the time I had gone through 20 or so college relationships with men who were weak minded, childish and just plain old stubborn when it came to following my commands; I realized that I would have to find a man who was going to be more sensitive and emotional. I wanted a woman with male parts! (lol) Truly though, what I actually mean is that I needed a man capable of understanding my underlying need to control. I wanted someone mellow and sweet – a dream man who was going to just let me have my way. I wanted to be spoiled and loved unconditionally just the way I am. You have said that before, right? At the same time, I wanted a confidant and successful, good-looking man. It is as though I almost wanted a metro-sexual man – sensitive and sweet, but at the same time that back woods boy chopping logs hollering, "Come here woman," you know, the type who can put a woman in her place when needed and give that strong, good love when we want it. This was really a sick state of affairs.

Finally, after dozens of painfully failed attempts, I began to see that the common factor in all my relationships was me. Maybe I was not fit to be a wife. My role models had experienced marriage and stayed married, but they did not seem to be mothering types. In fact, my mother was like me, really smart, beautiful, funny, social and very bright. She got along well with my dad, but from my perspective, it was clear that she was I charge. I could not ask her what it meant that none of my relationships were working. She would probably tell me to take care of myself and stop depending on a man for anything. In fact, both of my grandmother's, who each married at age 16, had counseled me in this way. They thought it silly that I even wanted a husband. They informed me that travel and career opportunity was the most important thing. They shared all the dreams they had deferred by dealing with 'those men', in addition to many lustful stories about all they would have done if only they had waited to marry. They said my career and education should be my focus. I tried to believe them…

Nonetheless, I could not deny this urge in me to relate with a man. My mom had married at 20 and birthed me at 23, and so I guess DNA would have me along for the same ride. Here I was 20 years old and ready for marriage. But how was I supposed to make this happen, not one of my friends had these same objectives. Everyone seemed content to party, date and focus on career. I wanted to be a mother and a wife. I was such an odd ball, but I was determined to find the answers to learning about womanhood, and realized I had to do it on my own.

I began to look beyond the books at the Howard University Library to find the answers I needed. I began to study Native American culture, African culture and Celtic culture. I read lots about the ways of ancient women and I began to notice strong analogies to the river and the ocean. I learned that womanhood is about being moist and watery. I learned that ancient women held families and nations intact by being feminine, peace loving and relaxed. I learned that the role of women is a powerful one that had been utilized over the centuries to grow food, heal people, lead nations and even wage war.

The women I studied also seemed to have special talents in the arts of healing, intuition, tantric sexual healing, and secret knowledge of plants and medicines…none of which had a place in modern society. The ancient women knew the 'spiritual' power of cooking food in a way to nourish her family properly. She knew to give the children and the men baths of herbs that would change their moods, and ease their minds. Ancient women learned these arts from strong bonds with other women, and were initiated very young into these ways. Women learned to use their connection to the Higher Power of the Universe to influence relationships without having to prove points, argue, get angry or become resentful.

So what did all of this have to do with me? The year was 1994 and I was a sophomore at Howard University. I did not live in the Bush with secret women who knew the secrets of relating to men. I had no idea what all of these skills that ancient women possessed could do for me today in modern culture. My own mother, and even her mother, had been a career woman. I did not really see what moisture, water and flow had to do with what I had seen my mothers do. I had no life experience that would inform me as to what it all meant. The closest connection I could draw is that my grandmother would cook and the foods and the feelings of the holidays would attract the entire family to her house. Was this a hint to what it means to flow and attract using the watery nature of womanhood? I needed to get closer to the real meaning of flow. So I began to visit the river. I went to the river to connect with the water that I was reading about in the literature regarding ancient womanhood.

I sat near the river for hours at a time. It was the Potomac River in Washington, DC. I could look at the Watergate building on my right and the Potomac on my left. I went to the river because I somehow knew that there I would find the answers I wanted. I needed to know what womanhood IS. I needed to get beyond my classical and linear training and connect to something more credible. I wanted my intuition back. I wanted my soul to feel open again. I was attracting men who were just not on the level that I know I deserved, and yet as broken, afraid and closed off as I was; I knew I deserved more. I needed to know how to stop attracting freaks, video game fanatics, weed heads, party animals and players. I wanted to attract my husband.

I went to the river to cleanse the old and invite the new. I wanted to find flow. I had no idea what to expect, but I felt a safe distance from total release, yet close enough to a new day. At the river, I began to shift just enough of my old hardened shell to open to true love. I stopped dating all together and began doing this River Walk every Friday. I had no idea that the River Walk would lead me directly to my buried womanhood and my husband all in the same year. Nor did I have any idea at that time that I would eventually revive enough of myself to write an entire book about the subject. My River Walks became more elaborate over time, but it was something I did habitually for up to five months prior to meeting Mr. Right on a blind date. Simply fabulous!

Process #1 – River Walk for Womanhood

Purpose: This is for women who are tired of being lost inside the mask of masculinity that schools, society and the expectations of our parents have casted upon us. This process will open you to love, self-love and release into the feminine principle.

Items Needed:
- ✓ Five oranges or a small pumpkin
- ✓ A journal
- ✓ A pen
- ✓ A bag to place all items
- ✓ White shirt and skirt or pants (optional)

Exercise:
1. On a Friday, go to a public or private river. If you do not have a river nearby, go to running water like a stream.
2. Walk out to a comfortable place.
3. Pray to your Creator about your request to unlock the Inner Woman.
4. Hold your oranges or pumpkin as you visualize what you desire in love.
5. After you have visualized and prayed, toss the fruit into the river.
6. Write down in your journal any insight or information that you intuit.
7. Repeat on as many Fridays as you would like.

River Walk Variation:
1. Pour sweet honey into the river to sweeten your life.
2. Carve the top off a pumpkin.
3. Place a hand written letter about what you desire into your pumpkin.
4. Pour honey into the pumpkin with the letter and place the top onto the pumpkin.
5. Toss the pumpkin into the river.

Meeting Mr. Right

After several months of not dating, because dating had become too painful, I continually spent my Fridays going on River Walks adding fun, self-loving requests to the waters all afternoon. I loved to make up all types of processes to expand my River Walk into something magical and healing just in the name of self-care. Each time I returned to my apartment from the river, I found that interesting things were afoot. One of those Fridays, I can home to the greeting of a tall, handsome man with nice long hair wearing a really sharp suit. He gestured to talk to me, and asked my name. I explored his physique, and wow, what a man. But in the back of my mind, I knew that he was not the one because he was involved with my neighbor, Alana. How foolish he must have thought I was that I would actually talk to my neighbor's boyfriend. Before I could call him on this, he told me that he wanted me to meet a friend of his. Oh, a friend! He wanted us to go to the movies that very next Friday. I told him that I had an engagement on Friday and that we would have to go to the movies late. I was not going to miss the River Walk for even a week and especially not for a man. As bad as I wanted a relationship, I wanted connection to my healing, Inner Woman first.

Needless to say, I planned to go on the blind date that my neighbor had rigged. I was not big on blind dates because I had a 'type' that I was looking for. I wanted tall, artistic, and eclectic and I preferred men with locs. But the river, I presume, had loosened some of the more controlling aspects of my personality, and so I said, "Yes" to my neighbor who told me he had the perfect guy for me. The river was working silently within me reminding me that a woman is open and sweet and is not in the business of control, but she accepts and opens to advances from men. She allows life to flow by without putting up dams. She is open to the energy of men approaching her. It's all good! Before the river, I had not been so open; I liked to choose my guys very selectively.

So Friday came and I was ready for my date, but I had decided that I would not skip a Friday at the river. I took to the shore early so that I could arrive back in time for the date. I tossed extra items into the river that day. I tossed quarters, five of them, and on each one, I made a wish. I wished for my husband, for self-acceptance, and three other things probably pertaining to the date. When my neighbor and his friend arrived to pick me up, they found that I was not at home. I was still at the river! Was this a subconscious control tactic or a legitimate time management issue? I do not know, but I was so late they left me. I arrived home to a note on the door informing me that they had gone to the movies at Union Station. I had no money to get into see the show because I had spent it all on offerings for the River Walks. How would I gain access to the movie and then find them in the dark? Without thinking, I trusted the Universe when it told me to go anyways, maybe for the first time ever. I felt myself in a flow of feminine force as I set out for Union Station.

Once I finally arrived to the location where the date was to commence, I found a nice male guard at the door. I told him a little white lie about my brother being in the movies with my car keys and that he had driven my car and had forgotten to give them back. The story made no logical sense, but my smile

41

did. With a smooth wink, I won the heart of that guard and he let me go into the theater to find 'my brother'. I found the movie we were going to see and guess whom else I found there. Yes, the nice looking man with the girlfriend who lived on my floor. His name was Keith. He greeted me and told me that my date, Carl, had just stepped out to get popcorn. Just as I turned to look at the entrance door, I saw a tall, slim man walking into the theater. It was he! But I could see that he was not my 'type'. He was someone who I could see dating for a while, but definitely not husband material.

I felt disappointed, yet at the same time just excited to be having this new experience. He seemed to be a different type of man than I had been seeing prior to the River Walks. His vibration was higher and he seemed far above the video game, weed, and player crew. While he did not appeal to the control freak in me who wanted a man who looked a certain way, he did appeal to the part of me – river walk or not – that saw him as tame, relaxed and easy to control. He would be my nice neat piece of furniture – moldable, pliable, and able to receive a little bit of good old fashioned coaching. This guy was becoming more appealing by the minute.

One really interesting part of the date was that this guy did not appear to be pressed about me. He seemed very confident and not too eager to please me. This was new. I was used to guys who acted like little boys by falling all over me and asking for my number at first sight, or telling me how pretty I was and gawking at my back side whenever I turned to walk away. This man was sweet, sensitive, yet alluring in his confidence and masculine energy. My inner femme and inner male continued to debate his standing. Was he going to be my sweet weakling or my dashing beau? His outer appearance suggested weakling, but his energy suggested dashing beau. Yooouuzza! I was going a little bit crazy. By the way, the date was August 25, he was 25 years old and I had just tossed five quarters (25-cent pieces) into the river. Not to mention I met him on a Friday, my River Walk day.

We had a decent time on that first date. The mystery of a new man was fun to solve. But at the end of the date, he hesitated in asking me for my phone number. In fact, I do not think he asked me at all; I was in shock. My rational was that his friend had already given it to him. This guy puzzled me. What type of man was this? He did not call me right away; he waited three days before contacting me. Those three days were terrible for me. I was thinking, "How could this guy ignore me this way? Who did he think he was?" I was a perfect ten back in my college days, so he should have been running to the phone to contact me. But it took him three whole days!

By the time he called, I was hot, but I was open. I was in the habit of appreciating a good challenge, which was another of the male traits that settled in early. I had learned to enjoy competition and chase just like the guys. This sort of competitive energy was something that my female friends enjoyed along with me. None of the women I knew wanted an easy man. Rather, we always enjoyed the most challenging, egocentric, bone-headed type guys. Were we all addicted to drama? Maybe, but I think it is yet another artifact to prove we are trained to be men. We like the thrill of a chase just as the guys do. It is not natural. This old habit of loving the drama shifted once I became more deeply entrenched in understanding my womanhood. At the time, I was stoked to find out just what he had that made him feel confident enough to pull a stunt like that; not calling me for three days was somehow sexy!

When he called, I immediately accepted a date to go dancing on a Sunday night. I am so glad I accepted without playing games. He really showed me a marvelous time that weekend. This charming man, with a tall, thin physique and preppy clothes had me laughing, dancing, eating and feeling like a Goddess! That River Walk was working! The way that he spoke to me was a complete turn on, he was charming and cool, you know? This one floored me! Not only was he charming, masculine and intelligent, he also seemed timid enough for me to RULE. I was also looking for a man who could bring home the bacon, and this dude was educated and on his way as an MBA student at Howard University. He was smart enough for me, and definitely not one of those dummies from the back of the classroom. Although he was masculine, he also seemed like the type who would never make me do something I did not want to do, or go against my wishes in anyway. This was heaven...

Of course, at the time I did not know that I was subconsciously scheming to rule his life. I was opening to the flow of my feminine energy. Here was the perfect male compliment, nice - but not too nice; masculine - but not domineering; smart - but just dumb enough to allow me to have my way. It was only in the back of my mind, or in my after thoughts that I contemplated the latter. I was not doing it on purpose. This way of thinking and sizing up men was subconscious. In our daily lives and our most forward facing thoughts, I was really falling in love. There were no bad vibes and no schemes. Looking back, however, I know that I was scheming. I had taken him for a fool, the perfect blend of trainable and rugged and had no idea that the entire plan, though not consciously made, would backfire in my face.

Even as I write this book, I am realizing how very silly it was to think I could ever have ruled this man's life and that to even try it would have meant the end of our relationship. But on that second date, my mind was racing with ideas and my fantasies looked juicy and fun. It all looked so easy; I had hit the jackpot!

Early in the relationship, I let this man know that I was really attracted to him. We spent every day together after that lovely Sunday evening. I could not stay away from him and he seemed to like me just as much. I was practicing my feminine flow and not playing hard to get. I told him at that time who I was, that I was healing, and that I was in need of real intimacy, even though I was still addicted to sex and had no idea what real intimacy was at all. I felt like it was safe to uncurl around him and into his life. I wanted to be vulnerable and for all intended purposes, I was vulnerable at first. He seemed to be so laid back and patient, yet I felt that he had a very masculine quality that I adored. I fell so deeply in love with the idea of having this man wrapped around my finger that I began to consider marriage. I had wanted to get married from age 14. Now I was ready and here was Mr. Right.

Of course, my idea of marriage was a myriad of images taken from my parents' relationship where my mother was a dominant influence. She had positioned herself well in the lifestyle she wanted and enjoyed many freedoms. My dad is an intellectual and college grad. He was strong, intelligent and fun and he had a broad knowledge and love for jazz music and poetry. I would go to him to experience a good time, but he was not the traditional head of our family. My mom was surely in charge. Her time in the American educational system having graduated Eastern Michigan University with a high degree was a factor in her approach. But her ideology on relationships was also based on a long history of African American women having adopted masculine traits out of necessity. Only problem is, the situation has shifted, but new attitudes on the part of women are slow to take root.

She had learned well how to place herself in the mother, as well as father position; for so long this is what each woman did to sustain their families in days of old. African American men simply did not have the same 'freedoms' as their female counterparts for a very long time. While I admire my parents and their accomplishments, I had to face the facts that I too had adopted my mother's stances. I was not afraid of marriage because I knew from my background that I would always maintain control, as my mother had. I had seen it work and I liked the look. I am from a family where the women hold dominant power and men just look good, give sex and go to work. YES! I plunged into the warped, outdated fantasy with the excitement of a young girl. I felt powerful – my River Walk was powerful, but the images from my past had more influence over me.

Weeks went by like days. This man took me out to dinner each night and kissed me goodbye each morning. We stayed out talking so late every night that our schoolwork began to suffer. We only caught up once we decided to bunk out at one another's apartments to get more work done. Two months into the relationship, I began broaching the subject of marriage more seriously with Mr. Right. He recoiled and held back like most men do when they feel they are being roped. But I did not let up and I was not going to leave this to an abstract notion like 'chance'. Sure, I was into going to the river and asking for what I wanted with oranges and sugar, but guess what, I was going to take this bull by the horn. I decided this was not the time for sweetness. I had learned well the ways of negotiation in debate club and college. I was not going to let this deal get away. After 12 weeks of dating him, I gave him an ultimatum, I wanted to get engaged and I wanted him to propose to me. I had the audacity to just go ahead and let him know my wishes. Just like that!

At first, my lover jerked about and tried to assert himself without losing me. He stated that he was not ready for this type of commitment although he could see himself being with me for the rest of his life. I informed him that without a proposal, he and I were done and could simply be friends, if that. I told him that sleeping over would be cut drastically and constant time together would have to stop. He seemed to understand that I was serious. After this particular conversation, I told him that he should leave my home and come back in three days after he had time to think this over, but in three days I expected an answer.

Whew, that was difficult. My Inner Woman was screaming out to just let things flow and trust the Universe. Hell no! I could not do that. The river was nice and flow felt pretty good. What felt better was control and taking a situation into my own hands. I mean what was I to trust? A river spirit whom I had never seen? No way! The river had gotten me this far, now it was time for flow to take a back seat and a huge reality check for my Inner Woman who was about to meet Inner Man, and here he was taking direct action, and so I did...can't play around with my life!

My lover left my house to return three days later with his response to the demand of engagement. In those three days, I cried my eyes out. My feminine nature had been awakened enough to feel vulnerable all of a sudden. What the @#$#? I began thinking that maybe I had pushed too hard – Oh golly; I was discovering I had a conscious. I was fearful that maybe he was going to reject me. Where did this come from and why was I feeling so crazy and out of control?

I had never been so open emotionally in my entire life. I would just let the feelings come and go as I watched. I actually began to listen and feel so connected to myself. I was into metaphysics at the time and I began hearing voices that told me to do certain things; they told me to pray. I remember sitting and praying that he do the right thing and just marry me. It was a very feminine prayer in which I used candles and was instructed to take a bath in honey and to use rose oils. I was told that my energy alone would help him make the right choice. I was actually using something other than words to bring forth change. I was not only praying and meditating, but I believed the voices in my head. I was doing the process of being feminine and it felt strange, but good. This was my first real entrance into full discovery of my 'other' powers. I had always possessed a very powerful voice to persuade others, but I had NEVER used prayer or inner work to influence an outside situation. This was the flow I had read about; the ancient women came to mind often, and I could finally relate.

I did another very feminine thing during those three days. I stopped by his house just to bring him lunch each day. We were both Howard University students and we had grown a tradition of meeting for lunch. When he opened the door to let me in each day I did not bring up the subject of our relationship. I simply dropped off lunch, ate with him and left. Femininity blossomed in the silence. Maybe he saw something in me at that point that gave him hope for our relationship. Maybe I would not always be talking and bossing and demanding. Maybe I had it in me to be a wife of dignity and light. I sure as hell was feeling strange. I ALWAYS talk. But I had been instructed not to talk in these moments, and, oh my gosh, I followed!

Finally, on the third day, he came to me. He asked me to come with him. I got into his car and asked him where we were going. He told me we were going out to dinner. We went to a very beautiful restaurant in Georgetown – I was closing this deal! My excitement raced as my body warmed to the notion that I had finally found my husband. Settled in our booth with lights low and soft music playing, I felt dreamy and I knew exactly what was going to happen. When he proposed marriage to me, I smiled with delight. The swordfish I was eating became moister in my mouth, and it all took place just a few steps away from the Potomac River where I had planted this seed at the river!

After a lovely, fairytale dinner, to make this thing official, we went to the jewelry store at the mall. He purchased my diamond right there on the spot! It seemed odd for him to charge a $4,000 ring to his American Express card while we were both still in college. Where would he get the money to pay this off? Not my problem. I could not think about everything at that moment. All I knew is that I had a carat on my ring finger just as I envisioned for so long over oranges and moonlight. I was so intensely happy and proud that I so easily accomplished what I had dreamed of for so long. And what a happy couple we would make. I truly did love him very much and I felt as though I had won a major victory. I felt life with him would be a cinch. I would just have to get him to see that everything should be my way and he would simply agree.

I met him in August, engaged him in October; nothing to do now except share everything with our families. A few blissful months passed and we decided on a wedding date. Of course when we went home at Christmas time that year, we had unexpected news for our families, we were getting married and additionally, we had decided to move in together. Everyone loved my fiancé and agreed that I had made a great choice. While although my mother agreed with my husband of choice, she disagreed with our plan to wait two years to marry and instead insisted that Mr. Right marry me in less than a year's time. My mom is a great negotiator, and the fruit does not fall far from the tree. So instead of waiting until I completed my undergrad degree at Howard University, we set the date for August 17, 1996, which was the exact date of my parents' anniversary. The legacy continues. Yes, I was good.

Once we moved in together after Christmas of that first year, just four months after we had met, my husband-to-be began to surprise me, and not in ways that I would have hoped like a little gift here, and a wonderful dinner there. But in other ways that would eventually unravel my perceived grasp over his mind. Sure, I was still in the flow, but the surprises he dished out seemed to snatch the thrown from under me and make me crazy with anger as he became unpredictable and horrible. Did he not understand that I was the Captain of this ship? Carl began to lay down the law in the little things that he suggested like the fact that he needed sleep and would not entertain me at all hours of the night. He also began to expect things like dinner and free time away from me at random times that eroded my perception of control. This shift was far worse than anything I could have expected. The entire pulse of my life began to move. He began to allow his masculine energy to unfold.

Damn, there was a MAN in my house where for so long I was the man. I would come and go as I pleased, I worked for no one, and my parents paid the rent and would send me money for life. I did not have to ask for anything from anyone. I dated as I chose, smoked my cigarettes, played loud music, and made love to myself at any time of day or night! I was extremely self-sufficient and I had not realized how much I enjoyed it until now. I merely thought that Carl would fit in with my program; however, instead of making love to myself, I would have a handsome man in my bed at night. I thought I could continue doing all the things that I did and have him join the fun. I guess that I felt his moving in would not rock me off my boat – it would be like a piece of furniture. I soon learned that buying a piece of furniture and acquiring a man are indeed two different things.

I found that my lover was not as easy going as I had hoped he would be. He would go along with my game of 'I want it my way' for a little while, but there came a point in every debate where he would assert himself and want his views to be heard and deemed dominant. He wanted sleep, not sex. He wanted lights out and quiet at night, and the bed made in the morning. He actually decided that he only wanted to go out once a week. Argh!

He moved into my place. My parents continued to pay the rent. This was my house, my furniture, and my grocery money yet he wanted to lead me. At least he wanted me to perceive him as the leader. He was a vegetarian and I still ate chicken and fish. He refused to eat the stuff and urged me to stop. He never said he wanted to be the leader and set the rules out right, but I felt he was trying to become the boss of me and through the back door at that. He never told me flat out that he wanted to be the primary decision maker. This hurt me so deeply because I was not prepared to allow him to lead me. My educational background and cultural training had taught me to lead others. I was not pliable or moldable, or receptive in any way to anything that he wanted me to do, especially if it even slightly went against what I believed to be true and right for myself. However and oddly enough, I continued to expect him to conform to my worldview.

His masculine energy was something that I had admired from a distance, but it began to buck up against my masculine energy. I wanted to talk about things and wished to discuss our differences all night, but he would tell me that the discussion was over and that he was going to sleep. I wanted to make house rules and decide on our way of existence together, and he would tell me he would work on that at another time. I wanted to set up meetings with him and deal with our schedule of 'family' time, but he told me that we could meet when he had a moment to spare. Thus, the direct confrontations began.

My River Walk had been powerful enough to produce a man in my life who would challenge me enough to completely uncover the Inner Woman in order to survive the relationship. And to top it all off, this behavior began prior to the wedding date. I was taken to the crossroads. The River Walk had been a huge setup! I reluctantly chose to continue with the relationship based on intuitive processes that only a woman can know. I felt that somehow this could be good for me. He was not hitting me, or being dangerous to me, he was not drug addicted or a felon. In fact, he was a vegetarian, a non-smoker, a non-drinker, and quite studious. The only issue was that he just would not conform to my requests in ways that I thought appropriate.

Nevertheless, we began to clash, big time! Our chosen stances were not polished. We had no relationship training, just somewhat useless college degrees that helped us not one iota in forming a workable situation in our home. The stories get wilder, the journey more perilous. But as each melee ensued, I became more able to see that we would have to do some major changing to actually survive this. And this is only the beginning. I will share fantastic stories throughout the course of this writing that will really paint a portrait of the average American young people attempting to create meaningful relationships in the face of overwhelming odds. Our sojourn together marks an opportunity to dive into a world of the under-equipped. Our life and times have been challenging and the road is just now easing, but only due to the understanding I share in the upcoming chapters. Yet, I am so glad we hung in there together.

It was not until later that I came to understand the value that these opportunities contributed to my growth and development as a woman. Here I am 13 years later, the year is 2008, and Mr. Right is still in my life; he is my husband and the father of our three children. Our relationship has been the only reason I have come so far in what I thought I could resolve in a few River Walks. I stayed with him all these years and together we have faced major and minor challenges without losing focus on the purpose of our relationship. We were lucky. Early on, we were told that the real purpose of a relationship is spiritual growth and development. So, by staying with him and working through all of this, I learned so much more than I would have if I had simply bucked him out of my life when I felt I should. Sure, we have been through many years of strife, but it has paid me all I was seeking – a deeper connection to Source, deeper intimacy with others, self-love, and true womanhood. But it has not all been a bowl of cherries! Does this sound familiar?

Directly confronting my mate about the many issues that I had with him and with our relationship, in general, almost destroyed us. Most of my anger was a result of my underdeveloped feminine energy. The River Walk was just an opening, which provided a great format to work out my problems. Essentially, however, I thought that I needed to change him. Changing a man is not the hard part; the challenge is that in order to change him, I had to first change myself. The first thing I had to change is my habit of confronting him. If I wanted him to be the man in my life, to consider my feelings, to care about my preferences and be kind to me, I had to stop confronting him directly about the issues. Part One of this book will provide examples in full detail of how fatal direct confrontation really is, but also how wonderful life is when we look at our relationship as a training ground for personal growth and development

Personal Growth and Development

I am only just beginning to realize how perfect my marriage is for me. It is sad that many people never expand and grow into their relationships in such a way where they allow the challenges to lead to personal growth and development. Most are too busy placing the blame on the other person to look deep within and find the real source of the pain. To change your man, you have to make pointed changes in your own character. Most leave their relationships before the force of dynamic change gets too strong. Few desire making radical self-growth the focus of the relationship, but I found that mindful and committed character growth was absolutely necessary in order for my relationship to work.

The biggest thing I had to learn is that respecting his wishes and honoring myself exist simultaneously. After years of battles and fights and all out wars, I am now beginning to understand that my husband expected to be the man in the relationship, and he expected subconsciously that I should be the woman. However, I was not trained to yield as a woman might, so I had to learn the hard way. Maybe you face this challenge as well. Adversely, I learned to think that my opinion had to dominate for things to feel right. I had to win and be right. Being a very receptive and feminine woman is not what I had been trained to do, so it seemed weak. Why should I have to respect his opinion? What about my opinion? I could not see how it was a 'both of us' thing. How could his opinion be important while mine was important too? I could not see how to approach life with him in an integrated way that oozed love and acceptance without me feeling castrated...but why castrated? I do not have a penis!

With all of my degrees, diplomas and skills, I did not have the virtue of knowing how to meet my husband in the middle. I had not learned that a relationship is a circle like the Earth, like the glyph for yin and yang, or like our very wedding rings. I had only learned the nature of conquest and personal victory. Schools rarely taught the concept of group victory or the win/win scenario. Maybe my penis was actually my diplomas and degrees and my independence. Either way, I wanted it intact. I wanted validation that I was smart too; just as smart as him and that my opinions and desires should be just as important as his. To follow his dictates without confronting him when I felt slighted or abused seemed so weak. Why not simply call him out on his stuff.

So what was I to do? I had to make some drastic changes in my persona in order to save the marriage and change my man:

- ❖ I had to stop making my opinion law.
- ❖ I had to stop reversing the roles in our relationship.
- ❖ I had to stop confronting him about our sex life.
- ❖ I had to stop controlling his comfort.
- ❖ I had to stop joking about his faults in public and in private.

It is called personal growth and development!

These are all forms of direct confrontation. The first five chapters address each of these confrontational styles and offer clear solutions to extract them from your marriage before it is too late. Once I made major changes in me, my man changed instantly. He began to love me just as I always wanted to be loved. He began to do and say all the things I wanted to hear. I stopped expecting him to become subservient to please me. He retained his role as a man, but he began to do it in the sweetest, most diplomatic ways. I loved this transition, but it came only after years of real work. You too can change your man easily by changing your own disagreeable behaviors. Whether it takes years, months or days is based on the amount of effort you are willing to put forth. Enjoy learning about yourself through the lenses of my own experience and please do try the processes on for size. They really help.

♀ Change Your Man ♂

Chapter 1: Give Him Common Sense

The first and easiest way to fall into the direct confrontation trap is to make your opinion on any given subject law, and run your relationship based on your personal perceptions and rules. Make sure you develop an intense expectation to have things go your way. Adapt the motto 'It's my way or the highway...' As well, make sure that your opinions are matters of sheer personal preference that you have stretched way beyond bounds. Decide that your opinion on any given subject is the simple and plain 'truth' of the matter, the actual 'facts of life'. Inflict it onto everyone, including your man, in a very self-righteous way as if he has no common sense. Treat him like a child who needs to learn from you. If he disagrees with you, convince him that everything must be done your way. If he will not succumb to your view, do it yourself and then call him a lazy, no good bastard until he can shape up and see things your way. (Please smile...it is OK. This is a real sad joke.)

This chapter is all about the kind of direct confrontation that is most usual in our relationships prior to marriage and beyond – our being too opinionated. The issue is that we often give our opinions stated as fact, but our intentions are pure, right ladies? We feel that men should wear a tux to a Black Tie affair, so we tell them they need to go and get one. When he states that maybe he will wear a suit and tie, we flip. Holding to our strong opinion as fact makes the situation tedious. If only we could see that whether or not he wears a tux or a swimming thong does not matter. What has to remain most important is the level of intimacy and love in the union. That is the point, correct? Basically, we want to be loved, honored and cherished as the woman in his life. Sadly, when we gripe about a simple thing such as a suit vs. a tux, we close the door on intimacy. We share our opinion in a direct manner and he takes offense to it. This erodes feelings of love he may have been feeling just minutes earlier and we wonder why he pulls away from intimacy all together. Of course, we blame him because he is so moody, withdrawn and sullen. But if we want to change him, we have to begin to hold back our opinions or at least stop making them law.

I used to make my opinions law so effortlessly. Let me give you a fine example of the way this form of direct confrontation evolves. This example is just a mild case in point. You would have to ask my husband to get the real juicy stuff.

Hotel Love

Some time ago before I was married, I held the opinion that if I am sharing a hotel room with a man, there should be sexual interaction and this was not up for debate. I guess I developed this expectation as I sat for hours watching soap operas as a young person. Lovers always took vacations to beautiful hotel locations where they made passionate love for hours, and then sat by the fire and just cuddled. I thought that the purpose of a hotel room was to make love. Most of our opinions and expectations develop in youth, but as an adult, I never thought to second-guess this view. Like many of you, I felt that this idea of sex in hotel rooms was just a part of me and what I preferred, so I developed a strong perception that having a hotel room with a man would equate to instant and wilder than normal sex. After all, on General Hospital and As the World Turns the women and men seemed to live in hotel rooms, and of course, were always having great sex.

Sure, as you read this you may think to yourself that this is not logical. It is simply a false perception. But it had formulated strong visual cues in me, and those images made deep imprints that became part of my identity. Images are very powerful; recall that in youth we accept what we see, and most of us began with the TV at birth as mother watched. Later in this chapter, we will do a process to reveal all that we have taken on as personal opinion and how much of it we believe to be fact.

As it was, my husband and I were driving to North Carolina from Washington, DC during a horrible electrical storm. The rain and the lightning had taken down many wires along I-95 as well as stopping traffic. My husband had wanted to continue driving through the storm, but I begged that he pull off. Once he pulled off the side of the road, we decided to stay in a hotel room. Actually, I kind of demanded that we stay the night. So we checked into a roadside motel, the Hampton Inn, in a backwoods part of North Carolina. Nothing fancy at all, but it was a hotel room and you know what I expected – SEX! Exacerbated by the fact that we were headed to his mother's house where sex was completely off limits, I became a walking pheromone!

We showered, brushed our teeth and tucked the sleeping babies nicely into their own beds. He took his shower quickly and reached the bed before me. When I finally snuggled in next to him, I immediately felt his bad vibes. His back was to me, he said no words, and his energy felt tensed and closed. I had feared (thus created) this moment; he did not even try to initiate sex with me, nor was he open to my advances. In fact, he went to sleep so quickly that night I thought it was an act, as I was very aware of the sleeping game that my husband played so often of hiding from me by faking sleep.

Allow me to admit, I was actually quite tired too. It was not that I was extraordinarily aroused after being on the road for six hours. The real issue was that we were in a hotel room, and my opinion or expectation based on fantasies I held as a little girl is that a hotel room is a perfect opportunity for sex. This fantasy had been poured into the metal mold that formed my rock solid expectations over the years. These expectations, numerous ones indeed, drove my desire and controlled my outlook therefore clouding my view. My masculine core was fixated on the fact that he was not responding to an expectation that I had. How dare he? As the minutes ticked away without any movement or words from him, I began to see images – violent images. The images suggested ways to jar him from sleep like storming out of the room, making a big scene and/or throwing a tantrum. Luckily, I had been learning to breathe, so I began to take deep breathes in and out to control these thoughts. My real saving grace was the fact that I was road weary and in need of sleep just as hubby was. But the next morning, it was the silent treatment ladies. I was not going to let him off the hook that easily.

The silent treatment is a covert form of a direct confrontation. I was silent with him and I had nothing to say when he asked me what was wrong. From knowing me all these years, he had already guessed that I expected sex, which is what had created tension the night before. His crawling into bed and turning his back to me was a silent protest against my expectations and a fight for his right to catch a few winks. I understood this and it was logical, but my Inner Male had no compassion for behavior that crossed the bounds of my expectations. My opinions were law for so long in our marriage that it just felt right to enforce them, even when they negated my own best interests.

Later in the car as the silence between us melted a bit, he admitted to me that he knew I expected sex. He insisted that it was just too late when we arrived and that he had worked all day, driven half the night while I slept. He was tired. This response was logical, but not the words that I wanted to hear, so I just glared at him with a sour look. I wanted him to apologize for not meeting my expectations of him. I wanted him to say he was sorry for not conforming to my way of thinking. His apology would signal to me that my opinions, expectations and worldview were safe for next time. Never once did I consider that my opinion about hotel rooms and sex were just plain unfounded.

Looking back on this situation, I feel so silly to have behaved like an infant with my mate in this way. He was not able to see that my behavior was simply a covert form of direct confrontation and a coping mechanism that I learned early in life. I was basing my functioning with him on the fact that he had failed to behave in a way that coincided with my opinion of what he should do or be for me. Therefore, I confronted him with a blank look and bad attitude. I made the car ride hell, and the best part of all is that we were headed to his parents' house. He was forced against a wall and would have to coddle me enough to get a smile out of me before we arrived. Who wants to arrive home to mom and dad with an irritable wife? Definitely not him.

This was just a minor incident that outlines the way that strong opinions lead to expectations of others, which can lead to disappointment and then confrontation. If I would eventually have to reprogram the strong opinion I held, I would have to change my attitude. At the time, I did not know a shift in me would signal and call forth a shift in him. Men do not like to feel pressured to fulfill a woman's opinions and expectations of him. Without this strong expectation for sex whenever we ended up together in a hotel room, my husband might have gotten into the bed with me that night and cuddled close. If he were not so fearful that this hotel room was a trap, he might even have been relaxed enough to initiate sex with me.

I would have to work years to stop demanding my way based on my own opinions of how life should be. I feel you may cringe when I say this, but maybe all women could get what they wanted from a man by realizing that just because we have an opinion of how a situation should unfold does not mean that our men have to comply. Using overt or covert forms of directly confronting him at first sign that he is not willing to comply will never change the situation. The issue is that having strong, dominate opinions and expecting him to follow scares him off. Men do not feel comfortable being around women who have strict expectations that when left unmet set her off. It is too much pressure. Sure, you can blame men for being weak minded and fearful of authority, but again, if you want to change him you have to decide that your opinion is not law. You will make him into a man with loads of common sense when you begin to trust him enough to make his own choices outside the influence of your strong opinions.

Have You Made Your Opinions Laws?

Once you begin to open yourself up to all of the possibilities of life and allow each situation in your home to play out naturally without inflicting your views on how each thing should go, then you will find that your man actually wants to please you. He wants you to be able to feel comfortable and happy. When you respect his choices and allow him to come to you if he needs your opinion, he will show you just how much common sense he has all on his own. Imagine that!

It is time for you to find a few examples of this type of direct confrontation and examine them in your marriage or relationship. Remember, we are looking for areas where your opinion is being inflicted upon your mate in an overt or covert way. Look deeply now into your own life. Get honest about your past. What are the expectations that you have of your mate? Have you made your opinions the laws of your home? Below are a few good examples of my opinions.

Work and Career:

My opinion is that a good husband should make the money and put all of it in a joint account where I have access to it. I also expect to be able to make most of the financial decisions. I want access to the cash and I do not need a budget. My opinion is that money is for spending.

Sunday Afternoon:

I expect to be taken to dinner and to spend family time with my husband and children. I really do not think it is right for him to work on Sundays. Also, he should not plan social events, such as golf, that do not include the family, especially on a Sunday.

After Work Activities:

I expect to go out to eat, especially if I have to work. I expect never to be expected to have sex after a long day of work. I want the house cleaned before bed, and I want him to be the one to turn off all lights, and so forth.

Vacation Decorum:

I expect my husband to plan a vacation for us one time per year. I expect him to dress well, be well groomed, and spend the entire vacation with me and with the children. I also want to have sex each day of the vacation, as obviously, we would be staying in a hotel room. I want him to show interest in me and talk to me. I want to be treated like a queen.

Now, list one expectation you have for each topic:

Work and Career:
Sunday Afternoons:

After Work Activities:
Vacation Decorum:
How to Behave with Your Parents:
How to Behave with Your Children:
Date Night:
Chores:
Sex:

These are general areas that many women have strong opinions on, and based on their own past experiences, these opinions may be so strong that they cause the men in their lives to feel trapped. My husband used to complain that I set so many unspoken rules he felt like he was walking on eggshells in his own life!

Once you have listed one of your major opinions next to each category, review each one more closely. Realize that for each opinion there are thousands more for each subheading. Then think about what your mate must feel about your opinions. How would you feel if you had to comply with another person's wishes and bow to their perceptions on how life should be? Then ask yourself these questions:

1. Have you and your mate ever discussed this?
2. Do you become tense when one of these expectations goes unheeded by your mate?
3. How does your mate feel about each of these?
4. Is he willing to comply?
5. How do you feel when he will not comply?
6. Are you willing to compromise on these?

Observe yourself and your mate the next time you are in a situation where one of your opinions is at stake and note the energies:

1. Is he tense or uneasy?
2. Are you looking for him to comply with your opinions and expectations?
3. Do you express your need for him to comply?
4. Is he happily fitting the mold?
5. Does he go along with your expectations unhappily?
6. Does he go along to keep the peace?
7. Do you argue when he bucks your expectations?

Look at the list of your opinions again. Place an X next to the expectations that he shuns. Place a check next to the ones he just goes along with to save himself an argument, and place a heart next to the ones that he agrees with and loves. Save this list for the exercise found at the end of this chapter. Would He Do This to You?

Finally, think for a minute about your mate's opinions and expectations. What if he was just as demanding as you are? Do you agree to openly heed all of his opinions about what a wife should do, how children should be raised, what

TV shows to watch and how to function socially with friends? Of course, you must have thought about the fact that he too comes into the marriage with opinions and expectations. What if he became just as hurt as you do when you did not follow one of his personal requests? And heaven forbid, what if he told you that his ideas were based on common sense? How could you debate with that? What would you do if the home ran based solely on his opinions and views?

In my experiences prior to marriage, I subconsciously longed for and had secretly hoped that my man would flow inside of my ideology and accept my opinions on life; think for a minute about your own relationship. Do you hold this misperception? I felt that my point of view was superior, and that nothing he did, said or believed in was right unless it coincided with my views on life. I had a strong point of view on just about everything. I wanted my opinion to matter because I wanted to matter. I was striving for power in the wrong ways. I was trying to declare that my opinion was founded on sound logic and common sense and should therefore heavily inform each decision that we made as a couple. It was not until I began to unravel this veiled lunacy that our relationship shifted for the better. I changed my man easily once I began to let him off the hook. He did not have to do things my way.

This was a huge struggle and not an easy transition for me. I used to believe that women without strong opinions were weak minded. I detested with a passion those dizzy types who seemed so brainless and indecisive, uttering silly words like 'yes, honey' or 'whatever you like'. I wanted to coach these women on the art of how to assert one's self and remain confident and strong. I felt like having an opinion on everything – learned early on in school – and especially being able to articulate one's opinion coherently, was of the utmost importance. I felt that by asserting my opinion, I would be better able to have a relationship in which the man understood exactly what was expected. Not only that, I felt that clearly articulating my opinion would mean that the man could more easily understand my views and conform to my logical expectations.

Over time, as my husband rejected more and more of my views, I had to ask myself fundamentally, "Do we have a right to our own opinions?" Well, of course we do, right? Funny, I never thought to ask this question before marriage because, of course, the answer was already yes. Please read on...

Do We Have the Right to an Opinion?

What I have learned in working through my marriage is that having strong opinions on everything leads to having specific expectations of others, which may or may not be soundly based. It is almost as if our net of opinions builds our own personal truth. To expect that someone else come in and uphold all of what we have become based on varied and personal life experiences is too large a request. I am going to state that there is a possibility that every person possesses his or her own individual indisputable truth. That truth is not a static set of social rules. It is more of an abstract expression of deeply individualized principle core values. So maybe the question is not 'Do I have the right to my opinion', but maybe, 'Do I have the right to inject my opinions into my marriage with the expectation that my mate must follow'? I learned the hard way that I could not hold someone else to one's own personal truth. I have learned that if I expected that my husband could view life in the exact same manner that I do, it would follow that he could also become a duplicate of me. Why not clone myself and marry me? Would I want to marry me?

The idea is to marry someone else. Becoming one with another person means acceptance and tolerance to another truth as it runs parallel with your own personal truth. And the fusion of the two truths – the many truths as they expand daily in the lives of each individual in a marriage – is actually the stuff that propels us into the future and makes us new every day. To become new to expand beyond old views and perceptions is referred to as spiritual growth and development. When one is developed spiritually, judgment of another never enters the equation. Judging others is the first mark of a person who has not yet evolved to the point of understanding that each individual is unique and that diversity is the divine essence of life.

So when it comes to creating common sense in your men, the first step is non-judgment...simply put, you have to release him from your opinions.

Principle #1: Release Him from Your Opinions

Do you think your man has no common sense? If having strong opinions, judging, and sentencing him based on your own personal opinions is the root to the problem, then learning to release him from your opinions is the solution, and compromise and acceptance of him as he is will boost his common sense. In order to compromise, one has to be willing to release the need to control. I did not know how to compromise. I was adamant that my way was the best and only way. In order to change my man I would have to concede to allow space for both our opinions to matter in the relationship and I had to remain happy with it. This was terribly difficult at first, but over time, it became easier.

Here are a few affirmations that you can say and use right now. I would guarantee the results, but the only guarantee comes when you are willing to change. If you are thinking that you do not have to release control and that control is not an issue in your relationship because your man needs your opinion to get along in life, then you really need these. Repeat these affirmations five times in the morning and five times at night. Just try them on for size.

- ❖ I am so thankful that I have learned to accept my partner's view, which is just as important as mine is.
- ❖ I am so glad that I have learned to respect the fact that I can only control myself, and my own emotional responses.
- ❖ I am so happy when I wake up in the moment and decide to compromise with my partner.
- ❖ Life is so effortless when I release my past expectations.
- ❖ I release my need to control as I open and allow myself to trust.
- ❖ All is well.

For those who are still unsure about what it is I speak of here, enjoy this next example. My strong opinion about taking out the trash is quite illuminating, so try to explore the situation further without shutting down and returning to your fortress of self-righteousness. The time for change is upon us.

Taking Out the Trash

My position even on very basic matters like taking out the trash was a matter of extreme importance. I felt that he should take the trash out before it filled and overflowed to the ground. That seems logical, right? I cook the food and he takes out the trash. My job as cook is time dependent; his job has a similar time factor. Trash stinks and fills the can after so many days. Children get hungry and cry after so many hours. Bed sheets get dirty after so many nights of sleeping on them. This timing of tasks is a part of my worldview, my opinion. I think it is a logical conclusion, but apparently, he does not.

His worldview is that he should take the trash out when he gets good and ready. OK, not so logical, but this is his personal truth, and I wanted to argue him down based on principle. Trash stinks so you should take it out as soon as the can fills. When I tried to debate this, it only led to chaos because his opinion was that the trash was not an issue. Why move from working and so forth to take the trash out just because it stinks? Hmmmm.

So what did compromise look like here? First, I had to get past the fact that although my view was logical, he had rational points too. He was never going to allow the state-of-the-house to control him. If he is working, the trash is second, if he is sleeping, the trash is second. On the other hand, I was obsessive and controlled by the condition of the house to the point where I could not work or sleep with the trash overflowing. So I had to look at that and see the hidden limitations in my opinions. Secondly, I had to accept that he was right and I was right. Uh oh, both of us can be right?

This went outside of my public school training where one answer was either right or wrong. I had to begin to think outside the box. Finally, I had to accept that sometimes it could be my way and sometimes it would be his way. Not taking out the trash on demand did not make him a bad person. Bottom line, if the kitchen smelled badly because of the trash, I would have to resign myself to waiting on him to take out the trash. I tried doing it a few times just to create harmony in our marriage. Lo and behold it did not kill me. Eventually, I bought several bottles of Lysol and called it a day!

You might be wondering why I could not take out the trash myself. Well, my grandmother always told me that taking out the trash was a man's role, which was another opinion that I was unwilling to release. Eventually getting a housekeeper solved the entire issue, which actually, we could afford because of my husband's excellent time management skills. Not obsessing over the condition of the house allowed him to be more productive at his work, which meant he always made enough money for our lives to be fabulous! So there, problem solved and how!

How to Release Control and Learn to Allow Him His Opinion

My trash obsession might seem small, but small issues get ugly when individuals cannot settle these disputes expediently. I could have forced the issue and made a huge fuss about it. I could have directly confronted him more often about the trash in an attempt to get him to do it my way. However, learning to process his opinions and dial back my own, essentially synergizing the two, became a safer way to deal with the problem. You too can begin to make sense of your mate by simply understanding that he has a reason for all he does and that the reason is probably a good one. You can both be right and create harmony if and only if you are willing to see that he too has innate common sense and is just as smart as you are.

How do you achieve this? Practice in your spare time. Refer back to your list of strong opinions from the exercise in 'Have You Made Your Opinions Laws?' earlier in the chapter.

1. Choose one of your stronger opinions, one with an 'X' in front of it.

2. Close your eyes and visualize the situation of conflicting views.
3. Practice compromising on this issue.
4. Say the words in your mind that you will say the next time this comes up, i.e., "What do you believe about this honey, why do you do it this way?"
5. Imagine your partner saying the words he might say when you compromise. Allow him to tell you about himself, and respect his very legitimate reasons for doing things the way he does.

This is an excellent meditation for your private moments. This is not to be done in the heat of a battle, but provides great training for those moments before they arise. This meditative practice will give you the perspective needed to resolve differences of opinion harmoniously. Let's now take a look at strategies to use the moment of a direct confrontation.

Release Control in the Moment of a Not-So-Big Confrontation

In the moment of would-be confrontation when you want to share your opinion and make it known what you will and will not do, use the following steps:

1. Become awake in the moment of a not-so-big confrontation. Maybe all of your buttons are not pressed, but you feel tension as he goes about a task in the 'wrong way'.
2. This should be easy; you are not that emotionally attached to having your way. This is just an aggravating moment.
3. Decide to observe yourself in the situation.
4. Remain calm; allow things to go his way.

5. Watch the situation unfold and find what he wants.
6. Find the good things about the situation. Realize that you will not die if this does not go your way.
7. Decide that you enjoy this new pattern of allowing your man to use his own God-given common sense.

In the Moment of a Heated Direct Confrontation

When things are really tense and you simply HAVE to share your opinion, furthermore you are angry as hell because he should have known better than to rebel against your worldviews, use this method…

1. Take a deep breath and count to ten before release.
2. Think before you talk. Never yell.
3. Allow your man to do things his way in that moment.
4. Never correct your husband in the moment of your serious internal struggle.
5. Once you feel calm, ask for a time when your man can talk about this.
6. When you talk, let your partner know that you are experiencing tension about this, but it is not his fault. Explain the way you are feeling and acknowledge that this is all based on your own opinion and that you are asking his advice on how you should handle this (after all, he did not do anything besides do it his way).
7. Tell him that you do not expect him to conform to your rules.
8. Find out what he thinks about your expectations, are they outlandish or would he actually be amenable to cooperating.
9. Allow him to suggest the middle ground. No demands please. Seek his wisdom and to compromise.

Let him tell you what to do and how to handle that situation in the future.

If you still have a hard time allowing situations in your home to work themselves out without you inflicting your ideas and determining the best course of action based on your personal opinions, you can bet that it is your own strong emotional response and ego attachment that stands in the way. You will need to learn to breathe and relax in the face of what you see as adversity. When your worldview comes crashing against his, conflict may ensue, and the only way to get above it is to calm down. It helps to repeat the affirmations daily. You will find that daily practice of this new way of being is what will tip the scales in your favor over time. Eventually, he will start to feel more comfortable that his opinions matter. Then he will appear to have more common sense than ever before! He may even take your opinions into consideration more often when he is not forced to live by them.

If you still want more, I have provided a very special process. This process is for women who have accused men of being ignorant for too long. It is time to change your man now and give him some common sense. This is strong medicine for women who have very high expectations and really need to shift the energy of the relationship for the better. If your husband is withdrawn, sullen, angry, listless, and secretive based on fear of your wrath, you should try this process. It will miraculously revitalize your relationship and allow you both to open to intimacy again.

Process #2 – Change Box

Purpose: Set your mate free from your strong expectations and opinions.

Items Needed:
- ✓ A picture of your husband
- ✓ A light blue candle
- ✓ A light blue clothe swatch
- ✓ A glass with spring water
- ✓ A small clear quartz crystal
- ✓ A quiet private room
- ✓ A quiet private moment
- ✓ A shoebox or special box of any sort
- ✓ A plastic baggie of ¼-cup sea salt

Preparation:
1. Collect each item (this may take several days or weeks); place each in the shoebox.
2. Place quartz crystal in plastic baggie of sea salt to cleanse and prepare.
3. Clean room, and plan a day and time to do this exercise when you will not be disturbed.

Exercise:
1. In a cleaned room, set the cloth on a table with all items neatly laid out on the cloth (except the shoebox). Place picture in such a way that it can be viewed upright. Maybe a frame will help.
2. View your workspace. Take some deep breaths in awe of the beauty. Make it pretty. Remove the crystal from the salt (discard baggie and salt). Light the candle.
3. Hold the crystal and pray for humility and change.
4. While holding the crystal, look at and gaze into the picture of your mate.
5. Recall all the things that you love about him.
6. Speak to your man's picture aloud. Tell him you accept him just as he is.

7. Apologize for holding him to such strict expectations based on your opinions.
8. Tell him that he is free. Repeat the words 'I free you' and 'I accept you' a few times.
9. Know that by freeing him, you free yourself and uplift the relationship.

   ❖ Meditate silently and just allow truth, love and light to come into you. Feel free to use inspirational and/or religious music. Hold the crystal and just breathe and pray.
   ❖ If you like, you can ask that the Universe show you ways to accept your mate so that the union can be peaceful.
   ❖ Write down any insight that comes from the meditation in your journal.
   ❖ You have freed the relationship and opened it to the influence of higher universal principles that will protect you and heal your relationship.
   ❖ When you are done, thank your creator and blow the candle out. Put away your work and keep it private. Repeat each Thursday until you feel lighter and freer.

You have several options for the charged crystal. You can place it near his bed, present it to him as a gift, run him a bath and place the crystal in the water, or you can place the crystal in your pillowcase. Either way, the charged crystal will act as a reminder that you are doing the work of creating deeper intimacy between you and your beloved.

Chapter 2: Make Him the Man – Discover Your Role

Wouldn't it be nice if you woke up one morning and your man was just acting like a real man? Maybe he is bringing you breakfast in bed, painting your toenails, or going through your closet with you helping you pick out your clothing. He may be cleaning the bathroom wearing an apron and deciding to quit his job and just stay home to pamper you. Perhaps he suggests a trip to the mall or the spa, or he is just so happy because you now give him advice, and hold him in your big strong arms. He feels assured because you make sure the sink is not clogged and that the bathroom toilets are not running. He is ecstatic that you painted the house, obtained a new contract and balanced the bank accounts, not to mention how well you are managing the investments you secured. Having life insurance, health insurance and stock options feels good to him. What? What's wrong, aren't these the things that real women do? No? Oh, well how do you know? Are you suggesting that there are specific gender roles for a man and a woman? You sexist person you! How politically incorrect!

Are gender roles real, or are they simply constructs of a society where women are subjugated to the boring stuff while men get to have all the fun? It is time to discuss gender roles and your desire to have your man be a real man. You can absolutely change your man in a myriad of ways that will allow him to show up as the type of man you desire, but first, you will have to accept that men and women are quite different, have very unique roles, and that gender equality is just not what it seems.

Instead of allowing men to be men and do for us the things that we actually say we want, we jump in there and attempt to do everything in the relationship, especially if we think that something is not being done the right way. For example, many women jump in to 'help' their man by working extra hours. Some women may decide that he is just too busy to do the chores he said he would do in the house, so they do the chores themselves. Still others may feel their men are not able to protect the home and secure the finances, or even manage simpler tasks such as order a movie or fix a snack. We would simply take over the task and chalk it up to helping him out. Yet, if you were to ask these quasi superwomen how they really feel about having to take on these extra duties, they might share how exhausted they truly are due to the bustle. However, at the same time, most of them never considered merely allowing their man to take even one of these tasks back without demanding that he do it. I find that most of us have not yet mastered the art of creating in our man a real man, as many of us are afraid to demonstrate that degree of trust.

The rub is this: by not allowing a man to step into the role of man, we hinder the natural process of his becoming that which we long for. In simpler terms, we want our men to take care of us, provide for us and make us feel safe and protected. Upon asking many women about this, their first answer is that they do not need a man to take care of them. But when I really probe to find the real answer to the question of what they want from men, they eventually open up to tell me exactly what I have stated. We do want, although with fearful hesitancy, our men to secure us. However, we have gotten into the habit of not expecting that any man ever will or even can protect us. So as a result, we reverse the roles and step into the 'liberated woman' act by paying half the tab, working for half the income, making half the family decisions and so forth.

It may take lots of practice to stop reversing the roles, but it is well worth the journey. Women reverse the roles due to a strong need to control and a sustained belief that men will never do it right. We bring harmony back to our lives when we release these controls and learn to receive. Will our guys get it right 100 percent of the time? No, but what do we get right at that rate? When we allow him to show his natural prowess without confronting him, demanding that he 'man up' or by simply doing his tasks for him with resentment, he will indeed get the message. Simply pulling back from trying to do everything will save the day, because then he will see that there is room for him to inject his strength and ability. This may be a challenge because most of us were not raised to receive in this way, and because we are oftentimes-natural perfectionists. Let's take a deeper look at the origins of this behavior and define what it means to reverse the roles in a relationship between a man and woman.

What is Role Reversal?

Role reversal is when the woman assumes traditional male responsibilities in a relationship simply because in modern society she can and therefore assumes she must. The primary reason that many women reverse roles is because they desire a better way of life for their families and themselves. Due to certain social conditions, women have internalized a belief that men are not reliable and cannot be depended upon, so quite logically and being natural born givers, we work to make up the slack. Other reasons women might reverse the roles in relationships is to overcome feelings of inferiority or guilt, to satisfy bouts of boredom, or simply to demonstrate their power and strength or mental aptitude.

Bear in mind, modern culture trains us to lead. Some say that women have had to step into a more masculine role to survive the world of single motherhood and dead-beat men. I can understand that this may have been the case in the past, but the future is up to us. If we want our men to be real men, we have to step out of the reversed roles and back into our natural womanhood.

At a core level, I believe that I personally have reversed the roles or refused to be in the traditional woman's role just to demonstrate that I can do anything he can do and better. Whatever the reason, reversing the roles in your relationship is an indirect way of directly confronting your mate. This is not something that registers on the conscious level, for I believe it is all unconscious behavior. No matter what the reasons are for the madness, when a woman reverses the roles in the home, the relationships between the man, woman and children are affected and become imbalanced. My mom did not mean to shift roles with my dad. She was doing what she thought was best, and I honor her; however, with the roles being skewed as they were in my childhood environment, I had lots to unlearn before I could have decent interaction with any man.

When a woman partially abandons her role in the relationship and assumes his role, she may chalk it up to the fact that the family needs more money, or the trash is overflowing, or she is not going to waste her brains in the home doing 'girlie stuff'. But it might all come down to the fact that modern cultural norms, which are accepted in childhood, do not support a woman being a woman and doing the things that women were made to do. Even as I write the words 'what women were made to do', I feel a cringe inside. We women are free and liberated and can do whatever we want to do! For we are all different and we were each 'made to do' different things, right?

When I discuss the idea that there may be natural roles for men and women in a relationship, it contradicts popular modern views that men and women are not bound to traditional roles in a relationship. Modern culture purports that men and women are equal. Equality in this instance means that we all have the same right to do as we please. While this interesting view of equality may work for many people, I have found that quite the contrary is true. I believe that, like our bodies, a man's role and a woman's role are quite different and when we can identify the urgency of both male and female energy to be present in any relationship, then we can begin a more realistic dialogue about relationships, in general.

I have found one thing that helps in talking with many women about the idea of gender roles. I suggest an intuitive exploration of what feels best for each individual woman. In this way, she can allow her own spirit to guide her in defining her role. Later in the chapter, we will discuss a powerful way to personalize your concept of gender. But for those women who complain that they want their man to be the man by wanting him to protect and serve, love and cherish, and respect and honor, then it is time to change your man. Stop reversing or dismissing the gender roles altogether. Steer clear of adopting his roles by discovering your own.

Further into Gender Roles: A Look at Physiology

Have you ever heard the concept of men being from Mars and women from Venus? James Ray wrote an excellent book on this very principal entitled Men are from Mars and Woman are from Venus. He describes the Mars energy as a masculine, warrior-type energy, while the Venus energy is quiet, creative and subtle. Venus is sensual and harmonious, while Mars is strong and forceful. I have found that this concept is also embodied in the ancient African and Chinese concepts of yin and yang. The ancients took the common-sense approach and based their assessment of gender roles on male and female physiology. Let's examine the physiology of women compared to that of men.

With respect to the physiology of men and women, men are very different from the average woman in many ways. Not only do they have a penis and testicles resting on the outside of their body, while women's reproductive organs rest inside, men have the capacity to become physically strong and can develop muscle to a much greater extent than a woman. A woman can workout like a man, but she will never become quite as muscular as a man, as the physical capacity is just not there. Also, the man's body houses his reproductive organs on the outside to keep them cool. Have you ever noticed that the testicles are cool to the touch; refrigerated by natural means. This is quite a handy design if you think about it. A man's internal energetic heat can go up higher than that of a woman, enabling him to do the heavy lifting, hard manual labor and intense mental work without causing damage or feeling the heat of these actions as stress or overexertion to his reproductive organs.

Men are literally engineered to be externalized and to participate in hard-core, physical activities that challenge the mind and strengthen the heart. In fact, men who do not use this core physical potential are falling ill in America to prostate cancer, which in my opinion, is based on the law of under use. This under use of the testosterone hormone (known as a male hormone) contributes to hair loss, prostate illness and depression. Testosterone has to be utilized in order for it not to become toxic in a man's blood stream. So in order to keep their reproductive health, men must include consistent cardiovascular workouts, regularly focused mental activity and lots of physically challenging competitive activities. When this does not happen, they develop blockages in blood flow. A block in the arteries or blood flow can lead to a block in the ability to have an erection. Men are most healthy mentally and physically when they are engaged in doing externally centered activity. For the most part, they are naturally impelled and physically able to do this type of yang activity...we can conclude that this externalized position is their natural role based on physiological science alone. By the way, on average, an adult human male body produces about 40 to 60 times more testosterone than an adult female body. (Wikipedia 2008)

On the other hand, the female reproductive organs are located directly in the center of a woman's body. She must take great care to keep her internal heat low and steady, as she is housing her storehouse of eggs, all of the future generations of children and the uterus, which holds the future of the world. That is pretty important. When I say 'low and steady' in reference to internal heat, I mean energy temperament. A woman who is cool, calm, relaxed and steady will have an easier time conceiving and holding on to a fetus.

Women literally hold more water than men in the breasts, hips and buttocks, and generally need more water in order to produce the extra blood each month in preparation to nurture potential life in the womb. If she heats up on a regular basis due to over exertion or stress, this extra water production is hampered and additionally can cause countless other problems for herself and her family. Because of this ability to house more water than men, a woman is also the element that allows water energy to come into the home potentially creating a flow of harmony. Most women most easily demonstrate this energy when they are in charge of decorating and cleaning the home. Her desire to decorate and clean is beyond the superficial. She is naturally a water bearer and as such can energize the home with a peaceful energy like ocean waves or river flow, which is one of her best attributes. Women also have the ability to feel deeply and intuitively know what is needed to bring synchronization to a situation. She has nesting abilities that far outweigh a man's ability in this same category.

She is the nurturer of new life and the only vehicle through which life can be transported to this Earth. American culture does not celebrate this much, so this information may sound new and foreign to you, but it is not. Ancient indigenous cultures all over the world have honored women for their power as the portal to life. Traditional women held special mores, writes and practices that portray these facts. Currently, celebration of traditional female power is nuanced and marginalized. Women like me decry traditional female roles, complaining that they simply are no longer valid and that it is 'old time religion'. We go about our merry way and continue to strain our bodies, minds and spirits as if there are no differences between men and women. As such, we lose out on the blessing of being informed and we suffer as a consequence. A woman becoming too externalized through over exertion of mental and physical activities can injure her womb and as a result end up with uterine fibroids, uterine and cervical cancer, as well as other reproductive illnesses including, you guessed it, breast cancer.

When a woman goes against this natural need for a cool, watery, steady and relaxed demeanor, which would keep her inner energy cool enough to house a fetus, she places herself in harms way. For instance, female athletes are having a hard time conceiving children, as many of them no longer have menstrual cycles. Their bodies have literally shut down that function as a result of the amount of heat it takes to be heavily athletic. Even women in corporate America are having difficulty conceiving due to the heat produced by prolonged intellectual focus. Another clear indicator of the dangers of externalization and inner heat is the fact that women are warned not to lift heavy items while pregnant. Doctors prohibit this type of lifting not because it will knock an internal screw loose, but because it will raise the woman's inner heat and her womb will not be watery and cool enough to sustain the life of the fetus. Of course, doctors may not make this connection; rather they state that lifting is bad for the pregnancy – sometimes they don't explain why. The effect of overexertion is energetic rather than physiological.

What doctors may not connect is that stress (mental heat) can cause issues to a woman's reproductive health. Women who are sterile have an internal heat that is just too high to sustain life so they often miscarry. This is why doctors encourage high-risk women to stay horizontal in bed for months in order to carry the child to term successfully. They have to cool down internally to carry the water energy a child needs to survive in the uterus. For this, I am speaking from experience rather than scientific data. I lost two babies while I was fighting my way through college. I was married and in my junior year at the university. With the degree of class work and stress I encountered daily, my belly became too hot inside to carry life. Additionally, it was this internal heat that caused my bout with uterine cancer. I suffered from the life altering illness at the young age of 23.

I survived, but many do not. It is a fact that many American women are developing fibroid tumors and cancers of the reproductive organs due to this excessive heat…my mother, sister and grandmother, all serious corporate types, have fibroids. I strongly believe that there is a hidden connection between a woman's internal heat and the creation of reproductive illness.

And finally, but most importantly, women who take care to keep stress levels low can achieve direct communication with the inner world, the world of spirit. Women are innately attuned to the inner world, which is why more women are found in churches and other religious places. We can dream and imagine and literally create our own reality. This ability to contact spirit, be intuitive, understand deep emotional issues, etc, seems to define our roles as nurturers and spiritualists.

The feminine hormones are what regulate all of these spiritual and emotional abilities, including conception, labor, birth and such. It also attunes women to the moon energy, which evenly regulates her menstrual cycles. Now that is quite powerful, men and women have separate sets of hormones creating general differences in their behavior. This fact of life has not been given its proper due.

I do not want the female liberation folks to jump down my throat, so I will not go any deeper into these physical differences. However, I will state that the Creator gave us physiological proof of our roles, so all we have to do is study science to know the truth of the matter. Do your own research. By natural law, men are to protect and provide for the family and community by using their externalizing gifts, while women are to nurture, bring harmony and are the internally (intuitively) gifted ones in the relationship. When these roles are reversed, serious issues are likely to arise.

Believe It or Not

It simply does not matter whether or not you accept this information. This chapter is about making your man the man of the relationship. If you want him to step up his masculine game to protect and serve you, you have to scale it back and be fearless about allowing him to do it. It is time to go ahead and become the woman in the relationship. Reversing the roles is a form of direct confrontation, and believe it or not, you must change your blatant denial of womanhood in order to change his insolate denial of manhood. Now your ideas may not be on par with mine, and that is perfectly fine, but what you must do for yourself is find a balance or an agreement on creating unity in your marriage or relationship.

We have to begin to allow him to do his job in the home without input and confrontation. We cannot reverse the roles at the first sign of danger and expect him to just take it. He wants to be responsible and he wants to do it at his own pace, just as you may want to use the information in this chapter at your own pace. How would you feel if one day he forced all of this new information on you and if you did not change in the moment, he simply started doing the woman's role himself? That would be a complete mess. But it is happening in our homes. I will share with you a funny and crazy story of a role reversal situation that I found myself in…enjoy!

Raking Leaves – My Role Reversal Mess

One day in mid-summer, I was outside raking the leaves. Why was I raking the leaves in mid-summer? Well, primarily because I had been asking my hubby to do it since the fall. And secondarily, I was pissed at him because I was very pregnant and wanted him to massage me, love me, and make love to me, but he was so cautious about the baby, and secretly angry at me for countless reasons that he would not give in to my desires. He also did not like the way that I had approached him about it. I did not come to him in a sweet voice and ask for these things. I approached him in a bad-tempered, sour, pregnant mama way, and when he asked me what was wrong I became angry instead of vulnerable. I accused him of never doing these loving things and that I was tired of it. Since men never want to feel like failures, that accusation immediately drove him into the cave. Many men will respond to a woman's anger in this way, because they want her to feel satisfied and portray great happiness all the time, which means they are successful. Her happiness is a subconscious signal that he is taking care of the home and doing his job right.

I was not thinking of all of the quantum physics at that time – accepting his bull was not my agenda. In fact, he was actually denying me the goodies based on some ego crap and I was not feeling happy at all. I was feeling out of control because I could not demand him to massage, caress and make love to my pregnant body. I thought about changing my tone, but altering my original angry approach would be admitting defeat, or that I was becoming vulnerable, feminine and receptive.........I was definitely not trying to appear weak. Webster's definition of vulnerable is 'open for attack'. I learned that in the third grade, so why go there?

Reversing the roles by raking the leaves helped. I was outside and it was a nice, sunny Sunday afternoon. He was sitting on the porch reading a book–stupid man. I hated to see him so calm. He was not paying any attention to me. We were both outside and he had nothing to say about the fact that I was raking leaves – his job from last fall. He just continued to read calmly on the porch.

I knew that I would need his help at the end of this project, since it would be difficult for me to bend down low enough to bag the leaves because they were too heavy and my belly would be in the way. But instead of calling him to help, which would be a further testament to my weakness, vulnerability and need for him, I just did it myself anyway. I bent on down there and struggled in pain, but I managed to bag those leaves. I felt the baby crunch in my womb and I felt the pressure in my head, which hurt badly, but at the time and inside of strong emotion, I do not think that I cared whether the baby lived or died. I did it, and made sure he saw me do his job!

I felt out of control as though he had all the power over my happiness. I had been asking so many times for months that he deal with the leaves, but he always had something else to do like taking care of himself and resting when not working. So as a result, I chose to do the chore myself; I stepped outside of my role and I raked the leaves.

What is the logic? I was proving to him that I could handle things without him and that I was good at it. Even in a pregnant state, I was stating by my actions that I could be more of a man than he could. I felt it most profoundly potent as I could jab him on two counts: first that he had not done the leaves, and secondly, he had not nurtured me in the ways I wanted. My head filled with evil thoughts, "If you want to get your dignity back, come on and get it, come help me rake these leaves, and be a man!"

After I had gotten all the leaves put away, I started to pick up the very heavy bags and take them to the curb. I just knew that this would set him off and cause him to click back into his manhood. Boy was I wrong. Even more important than reminding him that he had not yet raked the leaves, I wanted him to really worry about me, and ask me to sit down and relax. I wanted him to take over for me and then give me some much-needed attention and affection, maybe even lead to a sexual encounter. But he just sat there reading his book not even looking at me. What a complete fool!

It really pissed me off that the role reversal tactic was not working, so much so that the entire situation escalated and I got it in my mind to go confront him overtly! He was going to see me and acknowledge me - NOW! I marched up to the porch and began nailing him about the leaves and the fact that I had done the entire yard alone, that I should not have to do these things and he should stop me when he sees me doing his chores. I was pregnant for God's sake!

He said something mild in a calm voice, which I interpreted as a passive aggressive move, which resulted in my confronting him physically by grabbing his arm. He grabbed my arm right back (just what I had subconsciously planned–a response from him; an emotional rise in him, which registered as an acknowledgement of ME). At this point, a neighbor noticed the tussle, and my goodness she called the police! I saw her looking at us, but I did not expect her to do anything about it. Isn't this the way that all American couples conducted their homes?

By the time the police arrived, the argument was over and I was in the house crying. The police came to the door and told my husband what had been reported. They questioned him and came in to look through the house. They found me in the room crying and asked me if I was OK. I told them that I was fine. Subconsciously, I was hoping that they would not interrupt this process. I was almost to the finish line. You know, the part where hubby rushes in to apologize and then we hug, kiss and make up? I wanted to get my way after much avail.

The policemen told me that it had been reported that two persons were on the porch arguing and tussling. I was questioned; my report was that my husband had not hurt me and that the argument was over. I had to prove to them that I was fine and that I was safe. I never told them that I had started the argument and the physical violence. Men are the ones who are taken in the case of domestic violence no matter who causes the tussle. After discovering that we were just like the rest of the dysfunctional American married folks, or like they themselves having marital issues that no one could really understand, the policemen left. They probably had seen situations like this one million times.

Unfortunately, sometimes this is a dangerous game that can end in someone getting hurt. But not this time – it was finish line time!

Needless to say, it did happen, my husband came to me (points!) and he apologized about the situation. He said that he was not being as sensitive as he needed to be of me in my pregnant state. I was pleased and I felt a sense of power. My actions had not been in vain, however, the cost was high. The cost was not only the emotional stress that I placed on myself, on the family and my baby, but the unseen, unspoken wedge being driven between us. My strong-arm tactics of the use of role reversal as a direct confrontation were not endearing intimacy in our union. In fact, they began to make the energy of our relationship volatile and even stagnate.

True, my husband did acknowledge me in the end and gave me what I thought I needed, but he did not feel the sentiment deep from within. It was not the authentic form of love that I wanted him to feel. Nor did the tactics I used nurture him as a man. My actions actually made it difficult for him to love me. Sure, I could blame it all on the pregnancy, but that too is just an excuse. No pregnancy, menstrual cycle or hormonal imbalance could ever excuse this form of confrontation.

When a woman is pregnant, there are physiological changes with hormones and such, much like an exaggerated form of PMS. However, there are ways to manage this. One way is to practice deep breathing; another is to have support from friends other than hubby. Most importantly, the entire situation began because I was not in my role; I had reversed our roles because I was afraid of being vulnerable. Even my anger in asking for the special attention was a show of my own fear of rejection. I was directly confronting my mate simply because he would not behave in a way that I felt was appropriate. He would not give me attention so I confronted him instead of working a compromise out of love and respect.

We, as women, must become conscious of these types of direct confrontations. My direct confrontation using role reversal almost cost my baby's life. Even if your role reversals happen on a smaller and less emotional scale, they are stripping love from your relationships, resulting in your feeble attempts to gain power over your man becoming futile.

The Moral to the Story

Think about the small jobs. If you take out the trash when it is truly his job, you are stripping him of power and giving yourself even more excuses to mother him and consequently control him. Do you make the financial decisions, pay the bills, clean his desk, and organize his tools and the garage? Are you the primary disciplinarian in the house? If so, take a second look at this. Recall, as stated earlier, that women have to keep internal heat to a minimum in order to maintain good health. Even if you do not accept the physiological roles concept, if there is anything that he stated he would do, allow him to do it in his time. If you feel as though he is not doing it in the way that fits your expectations, find another way to deal with it.

Later in the chapter I will list many alternative ways to deal with these situations. But for now, let's look at another example of the role reversal game.

Another Example of Role Reversal

I dare say that maybe my above example is too extreme; many of you may not invoke all of that drama! OK, let me give you a leaner example of role reversal as a direct confrontation.

My husband drives me everywhere we go. As long as he is in the car, I expect not to have to drive. If we are together, he insists on driving because he enjoys this aspect of his manhood. I feel comfortable having him in the role as the protector and provider, and so does he, thank God! It makes many men feel good in their relationships that his wife or girlfriend depends upon him. This was annoying at first because when we met I had my own damned car and was perfectly capable of driving. I did not need him to drive me anywhere. However, once we downsized to one car and he became the primary driver, I felt like his refusal to allow me behind the steering wheel was usurping my power. Eventually, I learned to stop asking to drive because I realized this was something he was doing for me. A real woman knows how to receive what a man does for her...so I put the sword away.

So here is what happened one lone day. My husband and I were driving home from my hometown of Detroit back to Washington, DC. Against his wishes, I advised that we leave at 9:00 p.m. so that the children would sleep all the way home, which later proved to be a big mistake on my part. Six hours into the drive, my husband becomes very tired. When he began to look physically tired, I became very afraid. I did not want him to fall asleep on the road, so I stated my opinion that it seemed he was tired. He told me that he was OK and was going to drive a bit longer. Five minutes later, I repeated my concern, and once more he told me that he was fine. Since I was so sleepy, I could not fathom how he could possibly be awake and alert. I just wanted to fall into a deep sleep, yet each time I dozed off, I awoke in a panic to ask him if he was all right.

This continued for quite a while, until I stepped in and insisted that I drive the rest of the way. I reversed the roles and with good reason, I had been able to sleep for the first three hours of the trip so obviously, I it was better for me to drive. Instead of allowing him to figure out what to do about the ride home and to assess his own level of tiredness, I implemented my own plan. I told him to pull off and allow me to get a Starbucks drink. That would wake me up! I was a nursing mother, but the caffeine would not hit the baby until the morning. I confronted him with my plan and did not allow him to make a choice. Reluctantly, he gave up after I coerced him into compliance.

I got into the driver's seat and began to drive. After about 20 or so miles, I found that – Starbucks and all – I too was very tired. My husband had gone right to sleep and the three kids in the back were sleeping as well. I was alone and sitting in the seat of power over the family. The destinies of all of them were in my hands. This gave me a weird rush of excitement, but it was also quite scary as I found that I was dozing off while driving. I did not want to wake my husband and tell him the somber truth or ask him for advice. Instead, I made a unilateral decision to pull over to the side of the road.

Without thinking about safe placement, I parked on the shoulder of 270 N. After I had fallen to sleep for about 20 minutes or so, despite the noises of large trucks plowing by at high speed, I awoke to a flashlight tapping on the window. The policeman told me that we were in grave danger and that this particular 'pull off' was not a place to rest. My husband, by then, had awakened and was asking me what was going on. I told him what happened, and he just shook his head.

I pulled off the highway and found a more suitable place to rest. He was still in the passenger's seat, and it was I who felt the stress of dealing with the situation. I could have been relaxing in the passenger's seat allowing my husband to be a man if I had only allowed him to stay in his role. I just did not trust that he was on top of things, and I had used the logical excuse that the family might be in danger. Why did I feel that he would not pull off the road if he were tired? Why did I feel I had more common sense that he did? Boy, did I pay for that role reversal.

His testicles were over there cool as ever. Hell, they will always be cool; they are outside of his body in a mini refrigerator! He will be able to give life for a long time. Just a note in the case of couples who are infertile, it is usually the woman in 80 percent of the cases that cannot have children. The men are pretty cool (pun intended). We have to ask ourselves, why is that?

That night on the highway, I snatched from my mate the experience he could have gained in finding a suitable place for the family to dock and the feeling of manhood that comes with making a decision. I took all of that and had made bad choices and felt like a fool. He never resumed his role because men will not play that. If a woman wants to take the reins, they let her. Men are not to be toyed with in this way; they will not take the reins back without admission of guilt on the woman's part and even an apology. You may see it as small minded or immature, but here again is an example of the differences between men and women.

Later as we sat and slept in a safer area, I found that I could not sleep that well. The baby woke up and wanted to nurse. The steering wheel was in the way of a comfortable nursing position so I had to wake my husband again and ask him if we could switch seats with me. To switch seats I had to get out of the car and because I already had the crying baby in my arms, I had to take him into the cold with me as I ran to the passenger's side. The cold air was hitting the baby who was moist with perspiration from the warm car and he became ill in the days that followed.

I was just trying to help. I wanted to feel safe and in control, but instead, I gained a sick baby, a warning from the police, and sour looks from my husband who had not wanted me to do this in the first place. It sucks ladies to be in a position where you cannot allow him to be the man, where you feel that by stepping into his role you will somehow show him how smart and valuable you are – even save the family from harm. Please! This role reversal had backfired big time; it always backfires. It is not that my need to know he was driving safely was unwarranted, it is simply the way I went about fixing the problem that matters. If I had known more at the time, I would have expressed my concern something like this:

"Honey, I feel so anxious right now and I cannot sleep. I am afraid that you are sleepy and are not admitting it. What do you think I should do?"

It seems so easy, yet this behavior is foreign to most of us. By using this feminine language, women can express their feminine concerns about security, as well as their worries about certain situations without taking over and reversing the roles. It takes practice. But first, it takes a subtle acceptance that gender roles are real and that when we do not live by our own principles in this regard, we lose.

The Importance of Both Gender Roles

The need to reverse roles arises when we buy into a worldview that purports a man's external nature as being something more valuable than a woman's internal nature. This warped view on gender roles is a modern cultural idea, and is not based on anything sound. The law of nature supports the notion that women and men, yin and yang, and fire and water have separate, yet equally powerful roles. The issues arise when we are not educated on the importance of both roles.

The questions become, if a woman's role is so important, then why do we not see this role clearly demonstrated by our mothers, or on TV, or in the schools? Indeed, what is the role of a woman, and if it is important, what is its importance? Is it something that I will be able to do? Will I enjoy doing it, or will I feel like a slave? These are real questions that come up when contemplating gender roles. The answer is simple, if women are internally oriented by nature (physiology), our role must be to handle the internal functions. Does that mean that we should stay in the house barefoot and pregnant? I do not think so. In fact, it is up to you to decide what your role is in your relationship and as a woman. This process, however, must begin by accepting basic physiological insights and accepting that men and women are not the same.

Principle #2: Use Your Intuition to Determine Your Gender Role

After all is said and done, it is you who must define for yourself what you believe in terms of gender roles. It would be great to do this prior to marriage so that you and your potential mate can have a clear vision. As well, it would be great for you to have some ideas about what you are willing to do as a woman. It is like a job description for a potential employee. These are the duties you agree to prior to signing the contract or accepting the first paycheck. Just imagine how great it would be to know what you are willing to do prior to going into marriage. Armed with the Inner Wisdom of Self, a woman can go more wholeheartedly into marriage.

So why not take a few moments right now to do a meditative exercise that will lead you into self-realization. Repeat each of the following phrases and close your eyes after each. When you open your eyes, write a number 0 or 1. Number 0 means that you do not resonate with this concept or it does not fit into what you think of as the female role. Number 1 represents that this concept fits into your own intuitive feel for the female gender role. There is no in between.

Self Realization Meditation

- ❖ I am the core support for my family.
- ❖ I am the leader of the family.
- ❖ I am a devoted mother.
- ❖ I am devoted to my career.
- ❖ I love to please others.
- ❖ I love to be pleased.

❖ I easily and graciously nurture others.
❖ I easily allow others to nurture me.
❖ I am willing to support my husband's dreams.
❖ I need my husband to support my dreams.

Add the numbers (0) or (1) to see where you rank in terms of the three types of gender-defined women: the Real Shero, the Balanced Femme, and the Mysterious and Ambiguous Woman.

If you received 8 or more points, you are the Real Shero. You are the type of woman who is trying to fill every role in the family. Because of all that you do, you are probably exhausted by the end of the day. Juggling all the work and being both supporting and lead actress, you are probably considered very confident and capable by others, while very often you feel alone. You lose your temper quite a bit or you just hold stress inside. In your darker moments, you yearn for release and rest, but you can never seem to find a way to relieve yourself of the itch to do it all. Your husband has probably suggested that you open to receiving help, but his warnings fall onto deaf ears. You are independent and strong, but you thrive on chaos.

If you received between 4 and 7 points, you are what I consider a Balanced Femme. You are a person who is not too demanding or passive, but you have to decide what is most important for you as a woman, what you want to contribute to the family, and what types of concerns you have about your gender role. You are generally content; it is making sure that you are happy that is most important for you. You are a team player and you realize that you do not know it all. Others probably see you as humble, quiet, or reserved. You are actually quite capable of developing your gender role and willing to play your part in the family. All you have to do now is close your eyes and ask yourself what type of woman you want to be. What do you want to contribute to your family, marriage and to your own wellbeing?

If you received between 0 and 4 points, you are the Mysterious and Ambiguous Woman. You are flat in your womanhood, and charged with the mission to find yourself amidst a sea of possibilities. Defining yourself as a woman and working to carve out an identity will help you to unify in marriage. You are probably suffering on the inside with identity issues, or fighting old battles that began in your teen years. You have to decide that now is your time to define yourself and that it is OK to fall in line with the vision you dream of. All you have to do is close your eyes and work into your desires as a woman and partner. You cannot be wrong in defining yourself, and the definition will always be up for reshaping, but it begins with an initial idea – a lodestar for you to work towards. You may be damaged from past relationships or from childhood, but as you begin to see yourself as perfect with every experience you have gone through being one that helped make you into the brilliant person you are today, then you will be able to rebuild your identity and harmonize in union with another.

Using Intuition to Determine Your Gender Role

Now that you have taken the gender role quiz, you can explore your gender role even further by closing your eyes to meditate on it. We, of course, begin with the presumption that men and women are different, just as John Grey suggests in Men are from Mars and Woman are from Venus. Then we can move on to make an individual assessment of our gender role in order to bring balance to what society expects of us.

In your free time, you can complete a quick process that will open you up to defining and identifying that which you will exude as a woman on planet Earth. When you are ready, get your pad and pencil out, find a quiet place, and prepare to meditate. You may want to put on some soothing music before you begin. Ask yourself these questions, and write the answer that immediately comes to mind for each one:

1. Describe your mom (or primary female guardian) with three adjectives.
2. Are you like your mom?
3. Describe your grandmother (or another close female guardian) with three adjectives.
4. Are you like your grandmother?
5. Describe what type of woman you are with three adjectives.
6. Describe what type of woman you want to be with three adjectives.
7. Does your husband love the type of woman you are? Why or why not?
8. Would your husband love the type of woman you want to be? Why or why not?
9. Can you imagine being the type of woman you dream to become?
10. In terms of the woman you long to become, or would enjoy becoming:
    a. What does she enjoy doing?
    b. What does she not enjoy?
    c. What are her duties in the home?
    d. Does she work outside the home?
    e. Describe her attitude toward the children.
    f. Describe her attitude toward her husband.
    g. Describe her temperament.
    h. Describe her attitude toward housework.
    i. What does she do best?
    j. What are her greatest strengths?

k.   What makes her life so wonderful?

Once you have answered some of these questions, I want you to begin to visualize yourself as this woman who is truly your Inner Woman as described in question #10. Allow her out in your imagination and take her through some of the scenarios that you experience each day. How would she respond to the daily pressures that you currently face? Allow yourself to become her in these meditative moments. Smile when she smiles, laugh aloud and enjoy your life as this personified feminine version of yourself. The more you work with visualizing her, the more she will come to life inside of you, and eventually, she is you!

The importance of this exercise is that you have to begin thinking of the gender roles you want to take on; this is a personal choice. Think about the type of woman you desire to be and let the rest unfold. Once you have established who you are becoming as a woman, you can begin to define areas that you specialize in and you will begin to stick to those things rather than trying to do everyone's job in your household. Becoming your Inner Woman will allow you to take back the time and energy you are spending doing everything, or rebelling against defining your role by doing nothing.

Once you have done an intuitive assessment of your own feminine role as defined by you, it is time to make your required shifts. Whichever of the three major types of women you are, the Shero, the Balancing Femme, or the Ambiguous Woman, you can balance your energies by doing a sweet bath. Regardless of how you define your specific gender role, working on your overall sweetness is something that all women can do. To be sweet is to be receptive. To be receptive is to be open to the wisdom of Universal Love. All humans should want to be so open. It is not just a female thing.

It is easy to forget to be sweet, loving, and receptive. Women in this culture do so much externalized work by working just like men. I believe that this exercise should be done once per month to remind us of our role and the sweet peace that is a part of our role. This bath summons release of stress and openness to trusting that all is well no matter how things look on the surface. Furthermore, it opens women to the naturally existing yin energy in the Universe. As mentioned earlier in this chapter, yin energy is the feminine principle in the Universe. All we have to do is look at natural forces to find examples of feminine energy all around us. Maybe if we knew just how important and powerful the woman's role is in our relationships with men, we would not try to reverse roles in ways that directly confront our men. Be sure to take the inner woman you imagined in the above meditation into the bath with you. This bath will help you find the path between where you are and where you want to go. Life is a journey!

Process #3 – Sweet Bath

Items Needed:
- ✓ Jasmine oil
- ✓ Melon (watermelon or cantaloupe)
- ✓ Sea salt
- ✓ Nice bubble bath
- ✓ Positive written prayers/thoughts on womanhood

Exercise:
1. Choose a quiet Monday to take your bath.
2. Clean the bathroom and run a bubble bath using a cup or more of sea salt.
3. Cut the melon into edible slices and place near bath.
4. Place your written prayers/thoughts on womanhood near the bath.
5. Sit and relax, maybe playing soft music will help.

6. Once in a relaxed state, begin speaking the affirmations.
7. Eat the melon one at a time after you repeat each prayer; leave a few on the plate.
8. Sit back and relax; sink deep into a meditative state visualizing you as the woman you are becoming.
9. Wash your body with the melon. Yes!
   - ✓ Pray for a shift; ask that you be balanced in your womanhood.
   - ✓ As you wash your body with melon, continue to pray and affirm your womanhood.
   - ✓ When done, come out of the bath a new woman and put on fresh blue clothing.
   - ✓ You will feel rejuvenated and refreshed. Repeat when possible any Monday you like.

♀ Change Your Man ♂

Chapter 3: Make Him Romantic – Become Please Able

There are two types of women: women who love sex and women who cannot stand the act. Sure, there are multiple shades in between, but each polarization or type has the potential of making romance impossible. Women who love sex may not care much for intimacy, while women who loath the act may desire being intimate, but are fearful of it because it may lead to sex. Sometimes the answers to both are simple. Compromise, communication and understanding are the simple routes to healing a lack of romantic connection in a marriage or relationship.

Other times, there are deep roots to sexual problems that neither men nor women have a sound grasp on. Human beings developed these sexual personas from early childhood; rarely does the limited education we receive in this culture mature us enough to make an adult decision about how to sexually elicit the best response from our mates. This would require finding the roots to our sexual 'type' and then opening to shifting things around based on current reality thereby becoming please able. This section is all about the importance of becoming please able, which is imperative if we want our men to become desirable, sensitive dreamboat lovers.

Those of us, who are highly sexual, expect that the men in our lives comply with our demands and fulfill our every need. When they do not conform to our requests, we confront them regularly isolating them in our lives and tearing down all possibilities for true intimacy. The isolation happens as a result of them feeling attacked and overpowered by us. They fight to maintain dignity, respect and control as we castrate them verbally after we render them as 'so weak' as to not give us sex when we want it. They turn us away in order to preserve sovereignty not seeming to care about the effects of the subsequent disharmony. I have also found that the sexual cravings of high libido women have deeper roots than we might imagine.

Often times we are suffering from childhood issues such as molestation, promiscuity, and/or lack of attention from dad. In cases of molestation and promiscuity, we become dependent on receiving sex as the only form of intimacy that 'feels right'; we apply sex as a cover all for the skills in intimacy we lack or never learned. In cases of women who did not receive proper amounts of affection from dad, sex is used as a way of seeking starved male attention. Either way, the essence of our sexual heat is not altruistic. Rarely do I find women who simply have a high libido without exhibiting one or more of the above-mentioned causes, but it is very probable that there are some whose libido is just simply higher than normal; no doubt it can happen.

In terms of the women with a low sex drive, there are hidden roots to this as well. Maybe molestation, body image issues and lack of sexual education are the causes. Sometimes women who were molested exhibit a lower than normal sex drive. They feel fearful of the act of sex due to the shame and pain inflicted when the sexual violation occurred. They have never healed from the abuse and thus cannot find a way to explore healthy sexuality. Each time they think of sex, they think of the violation itself, which was obviously a devastating experience. Eventually, they may shut themselves off from men altogether in order to erase the memory of the past. Body image issues are prevalent as well. I once knew a woman who would not allow her husband of ten years to see her undress. She felt ashamed of her body and therefore was sexually inhibited.

Those women, who are simply ashamed of their bodies and their sexuality, probably inherited this from their mothers or from the environment of their youth. Many young girls are not taught that their bodies are beautiful no matter what their height or weight and that sex with a man is natural. I know a young woman who was actually taught that sex was bad, and that it would get her into big trouble, and these ideas stuck with her. When she reached puberty, her father essentially stopped playing with her in a loving way, and as a result of this, she grew up feeling that her developing body was bad and unclean.

Clinical sexual education, which teaches sexuality from a physiological perspective rather than simply sharing with young girls how fantastic their sexuality is, how fun and spiritual sex can be and so forth, fall flat. More extreme, is a lack of sex education period. This deters women from truly learning to cherish their sexual selves. Women who experience dysfunctional sex education oftentimes fail to explore what gives them pleasure. Finally learning how to have deep intense orgasms during sex is simply absent from most of our educational experiences. Why is that?

It is widely known that over 73 percent of all American women are not orgasmic. Many young girls are shamed into thinking that sexual exploration through masturbation is dirty. No one educated them about how to reach orgasm; to the contrary, they were warned not to touch their own bodies for fear of some religious wrath, or worse, they were fed a bunch of nonsense like 'masturbation stunts growth'! These women experience sexual shame, and thus, find it difficult to relax during the sexual act enough to experience orgasm.

Both types of women directly confront their mates when things are not going well in the bedroom. The strong lovers confront men by attacking them when they feel unfulfilled sexually. They make it all his fault and degrade him with words and actions. Do not try to mask it. You know that if you really want sex and he does not comply, you get pissed off. I know I do. I would imagine that women who are not particularly interested in sex become upset when men, who are physically oriented by nature, come on strong and expect sex on a regular basis. These women confront their men from the opposite direction and probably accuse them of being insensitive, solely sexually focused and having an overly aggressive sexual desire. Often, these women must indict men by deeming them animals, and shut down from sex. In both cases, sexual immaturity can lead to direct confrontations. Everything stems from both parties having a fantasy of what sex should be, but not being able to create that fantasy due to layers and layers of dysfunction with each one ending up blaming the other until chaos ensues.

Fantasies Unfulfilled

Most women go into marriage thinking that the sacred union might be the cure all for whatever their sexual dysfunction might be. Unfortunately, this is not the case. Usually things begin well, but then quickly unravel. We want our men to save us from our sexually inhibited or ultra-exhibited selves (my mom used to call me an exhibitionist so I know well that I am sexually exhibited), but this cannot happen without cognition of the internal sexual disorder. When sexual problems arise, we blame the man for not being as romantic as we imagine he should. But our sexual issues are not his fault and cannot be fixed by him.

Granted, when a man is sexually balanced it can aid a woman energetically to balance her own sexuality. But if we want our men to be romantic, we have to become sexually sane by exploring our internal blockages and doing the needed work to heal. Sure, he can support us through this, but usually this requires external assistance of some kind and much internal exploration.

A Personal Journey

Sex was something hubby and I fought about even prior to getting married. When I met him, he was 25 years old; I was just 21. I was in the summer of my sexual awakening. I wanted sex! Honestly, I truly wanted to be engaged with him on an intimate level one or more times per day. I guess I had a fantasy of marriage that was not in line with his fantasy. My husband is a hale and hearty type of guy, who is vegetarian and has a strong desire to feel balanced in his activity using holistic practices. Due to his belief in bodily balance and healthy lifestyle choices, he did not want to have daily sex with me; he felt more comfortable with once or maybe twice a week. His reasoning was that sex would drain him. He wanted less sex and he wanted me not to bother him about it. I did not know at the time that I was not into real healthy intimacy and that in my mind I had replaced intimacy with sex. I thought I was a picture of health, which is why I wanted sex. I felt my sex drive confirmed my good health.

I was confused. I had been programmed to believe that men were sex-crazed lunatics. I was used to entering each relationship ready to be the willing sex diva, and the guys loved it. Besides, sex is fun, and I have always been attracted to the energy and the spiritual nature of the act. I had never thought to take a second look at my motives. When I discovered my husband's lack of interest in my daily desire for sex, I became quite fearful. I felt as though his lack of sexual desire reflected a lack of love for me. How could a man who loved me resist my advances or push me away? I came to bed hungry for the energy of pleasure and he rejected me at least half of the time! Eventually I became quite sullen and then aggressive, and began to confront him about the issues. If I had simply given it some thought, I would have begun to realize that if I thought sex was love, then there was a problem with my motives.

The more aggressive I was about sex, the less likely he would be to accept my advances and give me the lovemaking that I longed for. Sometimes we would argue about it, exclaiming that I had a problem. At other times, he simply ignored me completely. He would retreat to the cave when I became really irate. He began to have subconscious responses to my aggression and direct confrontations. I began to notice that when we did make love, his erection was not complete; he was not able to last as long as he used to, and his ejaculations became a bit rushed.

I began to feel as though his actions were intentional. My ego was wounded by his lack of interest in me. It would be more than ten years before I learned from a tantric sex master that men often become erectile illiterate when dealing with women who refuse to respect and honor them. In other words, women who are aggressive, domineering and disrespectful create men who are lacking vitality in the bedroom. He educated me about the actual energy of the act of sex.

A man enjoys the act because he can see a reflection of his greatness in the woman as she reaches orgasm. However, if the woman is always the aggressor and she is 'doing her own thing', basically masturbating with her man inside her, the energy is diffused and the man never gets to experience his reflection, or his effect on the woman. He likened it to placing a penis in hot lava. Instead of the cooling moisture of a relaxed and patient woman, he experiences spicy heat – hot lava. The penis does not function well in this figurative environment, so the premature ejaculation is a surefire way to end the act and return to safety from the flames.

This would have sounded like mumbo jumbo to me back then. Hot lava my foot! I wanted sex and I wanted it on my terms. I was not 'doing my own thing' I was having sex! But what I did not realize is that my husband was not able to be the aggressor at all. Not only was I stripping his chance to initiate the act, but also I was bringing myself to orgasm instead of connecting to him and allowing the energy to bring me to orgasm.

At the age of 21, I was ill prepared to deal with this type of situation, and I had no one to counsel me on this subject. When I told my religious leaders, they told me to set a schedule for sex that we both could agree on. When we set the schedule, it felt as though I had him on a clock and the act lacked sincerity, which did not help matters.

This dilemma was with us prior to walking the isle, and ironically, we argued this issue on our honeymoon when he refused sex with me on the beautiful isle of St. Lucia. In fact, he fell ill on the honeymoon, so I was on my own for the entire eight-day trip! It would be years later before I would unravel this quandary. During all those years, I directly confronted him repeatedly about our sex life, and each confrontation sank him deeper into the cave as illustrated in John Grey's book, Men are from Mars and Women are from Venus.

After the honeymoon, things got progressively worse. I became so worked up and angry with this man for what I considered as his ignoring my needs. My anger and annoyance at him fueled the pseudo-male in me. So many fights ensued around the subject that it just became commonplace. Our bedroom was like a war zone even when we did have sex. It just was not fun anymore. I had sabotaged any hope for my sexual fantasies to live due to my confrontational style of backlash. Here is a funny story that occurred before we got married.

If All Else Fails Make Him Dinner

I distinctly recall a night in our first year of marriage when I really wanted to have an intimate experience with him. I set the tone by preparing a nice candlelight dinner, the house was perfectly clean, and I looked absolutely gorgeous. I applied my war paint – oops – I mean make-up, and I know I was looking hot! I decided that the evening would be perfect, no arguing, no tension, just the love that we had for one another. My hope was to rekindle the vibes we had in the beginning of our relationship, a time when I really felt he desired me sexually.

When he came in from his long, hard day of work, he was shocked to find my preparations. We ate the food and talked over the candlelit dinner. Mostly, we talked about my day, but I did have the courtesy to ask him how he was doing. He seemed to feel glad that I was asking him about his work as an IT consultant, as I usually did not show much interest. He also noticed the house and found relaxation in the environment I had created. Eventually he took a nice warm shower and got comfortable with me. I recall thinking the thoughts in the back of my mind…Is he going to make the first move? Is he going to reward me for this night with intimacy? I tried to steer my thoughts away from questioning. I simply wanted to enjoy without expectation.

I also decided to shower and relax to allow him some moments of silence and take a break from him to cool off rather than push for sex. After the shower, I took my body to the bed where I imagined he laid waiting for me to return. As I snuggled under the freshly washed Wamsutta linens, I realized that this man, my man, my darling husband whom I love so much, the one who enjoyed my candlelight dinner, basked in my clean spaces, the one whom I would not allow to touch a dish or to clean a pot, had fallen fast asleep; fast asleep! I was secretly devastated. I worked up those puppy dog tears and lay in bed crying, but my little sobs fell on deaf ears. How could he be sleeping through my tears? That pissed me off!

I tapped him on his limp sleeping shoulder. I viewed him as such a punk at times like this. I wanted a man who would be awake, fully awake in every part of his body, if you know what I mean, and ready to deal with a woman like me, you know? Just give me what I need in the bedroom. I asked him was he sleeping – a direct confrontation. I knew full well he was sleeping; he was deeply sleeping!

He did not answer me so I began to move around in the bed a little, tapping my fingers on the mattress and huffing my breath eagerly, until eventually, I turned on the light. He stirred but did not give me the attention that I was looking for. He just repositioned himself in the sheets that I had spent the day preparing. Next, I yanked the covers back intentionally uncovering him, and got out of bed – a super direct confrontation, and quite violent I might add!

From a dream state, he had the nerve to ask me, "What's wrong, honey?" I barked, "Nothing!" As a young woman, I had no idea how to communicate my needs and desires to him in a way that was not stiff and uneasy. In refusing to become vulnerable, I chose not to communicate the issues in a relaxed manner; I wanted him to probe more deeply and to show more concern, enough concern to appease me and help me know that he cared and would of course, meet my needs. He did not say another word; my stoic silence fell on deaf ears – again! He rolled over and went back to sleep. I decided that the only way out of this was – out of this! I got dressed very loudly and began to walk out the door. I wanted control of this situation! I wanted him to wake up and notice me, and care that I was pissed – opps, I mean hurt. Which was it? I just wanted to matter to him.

I walked out the door slamming it behind me. I had no idea what to do out in that hallway, and I was not going to go out of the apartment building alone either. We lived in Washington, DC and it was 11:45 p.m. The objective was to get his attention and force his hand, not go outdoors alone with only my agony to keep me company. I had to get back in there and make it happen...this plan was not working.

The next thing that happened is quite surprising and even I was quite shocked that I would go so far as to pull this stunt. But I did it; I walked back into the apartment, hung my coat and took off my shoes all the while visualizing this violent chain of events that made no sense to me logically, but if orchestrated correctly, would put me back into the driver's seat. You see, as it was, he had the power. I was the loser on the outside looking in. I did not want to feel so vulnerable, nor did I want to be soft about it. I intended to be heard. So I walked back to that bed and I snatched the covers right off of him. He WAS going to wake up and smell the coffee folks!

He woke in a panic and looked at me with a very sad look. He looked at me as though he had no idea who I was. He looked at me as if to say, "What in the world have I gotten myself into?" (We were not married yet – tee, hee, hee.) He probably felt disrespected and degraded, in addition to just plain tired. He went to work daily to make a living for our household. Although we did not have children yet, he was the center of our effort to purchase our first home. I was still obtaining my undergrad degree, so my life was less scheduled than his. He had to go to work in the morning, and here I was confronting him this way just because earlier I had failed to communicate in a vulnerable, loving way. I was afraid to let it be known that I was hurting and I needed him to help me and to work with me and to hear me. Of course, I could just say that. Instead, I proceeded to curse him out! I called that man every name in the book and more!

I turned from his stunned face and walked toward the bedroom door in a huff. I did not want to look at him. This whole ordeal seemed stupid now. It seemed as though my attack had crossed an unspoken line that I did not know existed until I saw the sadness in his eyes. Walking away, I had not expected to hear such a noise, but I heard a wiz wind zip across my left shoulder. When I looked ahead of me, I realized he had sent my favorite African statue – the three wise men – hurling across the room to strike me! He had intended to strike my head, but it missed. It hit the wall and cracked into tiny pieces missing me by only a small margin of time and space. I slipped out of the bedroom door and shut it tight behind me, running I guessed for my life.

He opened the bedroom door and came out naked to address me. With a desperate voice, he pleaded with me to simply tell him what the hell was wrong with me. In a sick way at that moment, I felt more powerful, and that FINALLY my actions caused a rise in him. I stood my ground and said nothing. I wanted more.

He turned all the lights on and looked at me deeply and with a strange sort of passion that actually I seemed to get a buzz from. He asked again what was wrong with me. I told him that I was sick of him. Now obviously this did not help to bring harmony. It was in that moment I realized for the first time that he had no idea what was going on. All he knew was that he came home to dinner and great conversation, he got to have some comfortable moments of silence and solitude, and finally he went to sleep. He literally had no idea that it was sex more than intimacy that I expected in return for the evening of fun. Sure, we shared intimacy that evening, but I had not counted this for anything. As it was, I stood clueless before his naked body feeling a wicked sense of power. Still I said nothing. Something in my eyes must have enlightened him to the facts, because suddenly it appeared that the light bulb clicked and blazed brightly inside his head. "This is all about sex, isn't it?" he asked with a look of surprise on his face.

Well finally, the dead has arisen! He spoke his truth; he really had no idea that I was expecting sex that evening. He said that it never crossed his mind. My attention to his words melted into my trying to fathom how sex with me had never crossed his mind. Fuck him! Could he not see my prefect size 6 body, beautiful skin, sexy hair-do and nicely scented lingerie? It would take a long time to discover that what he needed from me was not physical and had nothing to do with make-up, looks or clothing. He wanted deep sweetness and receptivity. He was waiting for the woman to emerge from behind the perfectly groomed body, but she was not there yet. Instead, he had the little girl still hungry for attention. In that moment, I felt the tinge of his seething hurt and overwhelming dissolution. If my ego had not stepped in to take up for me, I would have fallen apart right there.

Instead of being vulnerable when the tears came, and running to his arms for real comfort from the pain, I allowed the tears to signify my anger. Through hot tears and fast heaving, I called him a liar. I told him how much I hated the fact that he was not man enough to know when a woman needed some dick! I called him a faggot and I told him to fuck off! I turned to move away from his glance. Totally embarrassed, I could not reveal the fact that his lack of interest was hurting me so deeply.

He could not see that his actions were mimicking the lack of attention that I received from the men who raised me. The lack of hugs, attention, and affection from all the men in my family and extended family were present in that moment, and here I was, defending that little girl. He could not see that youthful me as I stood poised to throw the tantrum that I wanted to as a girl. I think I was screaming insults, but I cannot recall. I had collapsed into my own emotional black hole of the past and was not even present in my body to know the difference between him and the men who had ignored me.

He immediately got dressed and began to leave the house. He was not going to stay in the house and be spoken to in that manner. Men are not as comfortable with this strong emotional thing as women are. He could not go there with me. Men honestly believe that they could die from exposure to this realm of emotional drama. It is so true! He got dressed quickly and began to walk out the front door.

Oh hell no, I was not having that! I came out of trance and took action. He was pulling a power move during the middle of this discussion, and I sure as hell was not going to allow it. I wanted the power, plus, this was my show. For all intensive purposes, he was asleep just five minutes ago! How dare he think he was going to wake up, try to kill me with a wooden statue, utter a few caring words and then leave me here alone? I had to act quickly and think of the next plan of attack.

I stood in front of the door and told him that he was not going to leave the house. He pushed me out of the way and a tussle began. I locked the door so that he could not leave. He unlocked the door. I tried to stop him. Pushing my smaller body out of the way, he left anyways. Into the apartment hallway he went headed for the elevator. I knew that old elevator was slow and I could catch him, but I needed the right dramatic weapon to prove that I was serious. I went to the kitchen and pondered the choice of utensil. Eventually, I grabbed the first weapon I could find – a steak knife – and went after him. I had no intention of hurting him. I only wanted to make an impression; show him how serious I was about this.

He was standing at the elevator when I came into the hallway half dressed in odd clothing and an old sweater. The elevator door opened, someone was in there – shit! I pulled the knife up into my sleeve and followed him into the elevator. I hated to make a public scene, so I used a voice that was feminine and vulnerable when I asked him to please come back home. How fake. Why was I not able to use this sweet voice in our home prior to the drama? I do not know. But in the elevator and in front of others, I was on my best behavior. He replied to my false femme with a rude and loud, "Hell no!"

The elevator door opened to the lobby and I waved happily at the doorman and smiled sweetly at the attendant. The knife was out of view, flipped upside down with the blade in the sleeve of my sweater. I followed my husband who was walking at a quick pace down Euclid Street headed toward Georgia Avenue. He walked at least a half-mile and I followed him all the way. Along the path, we saw the many vagrants who must hang out like this every night, I guessed. Funny, we fit right in although we were collegiate students, the talented tenth, residing in the Nation's Capital for the purpose of attending University. Our fine education should have also included relationships 101 and definitely marriage 101 because we were bucking wild in this thing.

I found myself yelling at him to come back, wait for me and let's talk. I warned him that if he did not come home that someone was going to get hurt. He did not respond to me; he kept walking. What was I going to do with the knife? I was thinking on that. I needed to devise a plan.

What fools we must have appeared to be to passersby. Maybe we looked like so many other crack fiends scampering across the avenue in the wee hours of the night...I felt very much like a fiend of some sort craving some sort of high; addicted to the drama of confrontation and to the melodrama of making up.

Oddly enough, a police car began to follow us as I suspect we must have looked quite suspicious walking fast, power walking at midnight on the DC streets. The vagrants did not walk so fast so we must have stood out like sore thumbs, me with a knife in plain view and him looking so angry and intense. I cannot blame him for being out of sorts, I mean; he had no idea what I was capable of doing. I had done some real shit in my day.

The police pulled up next to him and shined a flashlight out the window at his face. This gave me a chance to catch up to him. They asked him if he was all right. He told them he was OK, and then pointed back at me. "She is the one who is not OK," he told the police. "She is one crazy bitch." Oh man, he busted me out! I had been crying all night, my eyes must have been as red as a wino's. I probably looked high, when drugs were the farthest things from my mind. And, oh my gosh, the knife! I had the stupid knife in my hand. What if the police found that?

The flashlight hit my eyes and I winced. The policeman asked me if everything was OK. I said, "Yes, fine..." They kind of looked at him and then back at me, and it all registered – these two kids must be in love. They asked if we needed help, when I am sure in their minds we were just like the thousands of young lovers they had seen probably strolling in the streets at midnight trying to settle issues in obscene ways just like us. Why were policemen so used to this sort of scene? Couples so much in love, but with no clue as to how to relate, communicate or compromise. So we were just another set of kids trying to figure out love alone. The policeman rode away slowly making tickled, snickering noises at us.

But aha! I had caught up to him, and I had his hand so he could not run away from me this time. I had caught his ass! How sick was I! This was actually a victory for me, so no more need to fight. I had released enough tension and caused enough pain; I could finally come to my senses and talk to him about the issue. It was only after wild fits of anger and pain that I could talk with sense. I had to drive him nuts before I actually broke down and shared in any acceptable format.

Maybe I felt as though I had wielded my power and that his hand had been forced. It gave me satisfaction that at least I got my power back. To be vulnerable before trapping him in my emotional web seemed dangerous and frightening. It would take time to realize that this was not the best way to conduct a marriage, and that I would have to forget about winning power battles if my marriage was going to last.

Finally, in an authentic feminine voice and with real openness, I told him that I had composed the entire evening for him, and that I wanted to relax him so that he could initiate sex with me. I told him my plan to set everything up, but not mention sex at all, was so that he could be the clear aggressor. I was tired of always being the sexual aggressor; I needed to feel his desire for me. I was trying an experiment and it had all backfired.

After catching his breath and taking some moments of silence, he informed me that he had no idea I wanted sex at the end of the evening. He was simply enjoying the space and relaxing his mind. He was tired for goodness sake. He was hurt that I had expected him to read my mind. He actually thought that I had finally given nod to the fact that he was working too hard and needed my support at home. He thought the candlelight dinner was something I was doing to nurture him; you know, care for his needs woman to man.

How wrong he was. Nurture him? Care for his needs? I was not thinking about providing something just for HIM. I only masked my intentions so that it would appear that way. What I was doing at that time was something for me. Looking back, I might have deemed it an act of love and really defended myself to prove that it was love based. I would probably have told my friends all about how I slaved for him in the kitchen and then cleaned the house for what, to get a statue tossed at my head and walk the streets of DC chasing him all night? They would have agreed that men are really stupid! None of my friends had the experience or judgment to help me out of this.

In no way was this plan working for me; eventually, I felt totally out of control. Then I became angry and needed to do something drastic to gain control back again; hence, another direct confrontation; an ugly cycle. My confrontations with my husband were what drove the wedge between us. In retrospect, my inability to note my own sexual dysfunction is clear. I used to think all of this was cute. Imagine that?

Even as I was able to become vulnerable and share my truest intentions, in the end, he still did not warm up to me or take me home to give me what I demanded. Rather, we walked home in peace and went to sleep in separate rooms. I had the notion at that time that he could not love me right. I thought he just was not romantic, and I blamed him secretly for the entire thing. Boy was I wrong; he loved me very much and he was willing to hang in there with me and never once did he leave me even after the most serious battles – this not being one of them.

What man wants to make love to a hot, angry tangle of negative emotional energy? It would not be until I went to the core of my being and began to dismantle the imbalanced male forces inside of me resulting from the pain in my childhood that I could even expect him to open to me in the romantic ways I desired. Maybe I could have given him a bath, told him with a sweet voice that I was in need of his manhood; I was in need of a man's hands, a man's touch, and a man's appreciation of a woman. But I would have to first be a woman to communicate this…my anger prevented it. An angry woman just is not appealing to a man. I could never make him romantic by getting angry. An angry woman is not a please able woman by any means.

Allow Pleasure – Be Please Able

OK, so are you really ready to change your man into a romantic warrior and excellent lover? The key to unlock a man's romance is really quite simple. We must become please able. What does this mean, and how does it apply to any relationship? The route that I took in directly confronting my man about sex is one that many women take. We simply confront the man with anger, even rage when we feel unfulfilled. If a woman does not enjoy sex and wants less of it, she overtly confronts her man by saying no, faking illness, implying no, or just going to sleep each night without a peep.

In either case, the woman's confrontation of the man only fuels the fire. The woman who wants less sex or is frigid will isolate her mate by her lack of interest. The woman who wants more and better sex isolates her mate with her disrespectful responses to his refusal. In both situations, the woman is not being please able. A man feels terrible when he cannot please his woman simply by being whom he is and how he is sexually. Men feel the sting of failure so much more poignantly than women do; every book on relationships that I have studied correlates the male energy to that which wants to succeed. Men want to be successful, and revered and honored as such. When they feel as though they are successful, they are more likely to try even harder to please women. This translates in terms of sexual relationships this way: the man who is motivated to please his woman in a sensitive and romantic way knows in advance that his woman is pleased by him. The motivation deepens each time she expresses acceptance of his sexual energy.

Therein lays the key to a man's heart! If you want him to please you sexually, let him succeed. Sure you have to work on your internal pain and sexual conditionings as you go, but once you get a handle on your own hurt feelings or mistreatment from childhood, you can open to accepting your man's sexual self. Do not worry; I readily acknowledge that men have sexual issues too. But as you work your issues out, he too will internally work his own issues out. Meanwhile, he wants to succeed sexually, so let him succeed! Your please ability will train him to be romantic and sensitive. It is so easy! I know it is a deep concept, but don't worry I will explain, and you will soon find the ease of using this little key to make your man just as romantic and sweet as you would like.

Principle #3: Be Pleased By Every Intimate Action He Initiates

As I mentioned earlier, it was not until dealing with a Tantra master that I even learned the concept of being please able. My mother never taught me this magic, no one taught her either. Being please able simply means that as a woman, no matter which sexual type you are, you send positive messages to your man when he is exhibiting his sexual self. Many believe that it is not right to become please able if it is not sincere. However, I dare say that learning to be please able is a principle steeped in metaphysical significance and will transfer to vast personal development and acquisition of all that we desire. Being please able is another way of showing appreciation for what is with the expectation that things will improve over time.

The importance of even exploring this exercise is that everything happens for a reason. Like attracts like and opposites attract. We have chosen our current partners for many reasons. In particular, we often choose our partners to help us open to new and hidden sexual possibilities that without him/her we never would attain. If you have a high libido and your man is puttering, you are in the relationship to find the middle path and walk it. If you have a low libido and your man is a sexual maniac, you are learning to raise your energy to meet the middle ground and stand it happily. You are with him to grow yourself and your character and to learn to harmonize with another person on planet Earth.

The requirement to become please able would be that you decide right now to allow his every effort to please you, no matter what! Yes, even the things that piss you off like him reaching out to touch your butt in public, or him desiring a kiss when you are in the middle of cooking dinner. The wise ones say that whatever pisses you the hell off is where your work on this Earth resides. Wayne Dyer calls it the Earth School. We are here to realize our full potential, but this will never happen if we naturally chose mates that are just the same as we are. Almost always the case is that we are mated with persons who will challenge who we think we are.

When we choose to be at peace when he exhibits his sexual self, we learn who we are. If we find that we become pissed when he tries to kiss us when we are busy, we learn that we have certain walls up and that limit our capacity for receiving love. Essentially, we want to control issues around sex. To pretend as though the kiss is not an issue and instead choose to be pleased by the act, we thereby begin to cancel whatever negative blockages exist between intimacy and us. The real question becomes, why does a kiss at the 'wrong time' bother you? The answer to this question is vastly more important that it seems.

Childhood traumas, blocks to intimacy, and so forth, have to be worked out; we are not on Earth to hold on to the past forever. There is deep meaning to the events that took place in our sexual histories. To unravel them we have to go through the perceived pain, become cognizant of our motives and shift our behaviors. Intimacy works in a way that lures us into wanting more of it, but it cannot always be on our terms. Learning to receive it in broader terms will grow us immeasurably. And when we practice receiving his sexual energy and being pleased by it, no matter what or when, we unlearn whatever responses of old we have clung to as protection all these years.

Now I know some of you are probably saying that this is all too female based. Why can't he pretend to be pleased by us? Why can't he decide that whatever we do he will receive it and enjoy it? Well, this book is about changing your man. If you want him to become this type: sensitive, sweet, please able and romantic, YOU have to exhibit this. We cannot attract what we are not, and we definitely cannot have what we are not. So becoming this type of intimate receptor will allow you to attract his romantic side. Oh believe me, it is there! Unfortunately, however, it is set to function in the ways you currently receive it. If you push it away and call it bad names, it responds as a bad boy, just as you expect. But when you begin to embrace his sexual side and tell it how good it is, it will respond by being good to you and giving you all that you expect to receive.

So in terms of being please able, this is the key to creating the love you desire. It is the only key that will unlock your man's heart and make him the romantic person that you dream of him being. To become please able means that you must relish in his love no matter what. Even something as simple as his patting you on the butt – gross to some, pleasing to others, or giving you a peck on the check – too light for some, too heavy for others.

Begin to ravish and adore all forms of love he gives you. Let these small gestures excite you and express your pleasure openly to him. Fake it 'til you make it girl! Just imagine what would have happened during my candlelight dinner party if I had relished in the fact that my man was home with me, enjoying my food, sitting at the table with me, and willing to lay down and sleep near me desiring only to cuddle in my arms. At the time, it was a bit too weak for me, but what if I could have chosen to be pleased by it, deciding it would have been enough?

Hang in here with me a moment ladies; I know this is not easy, but the rewards are fabulous! I will be giving you some sweet affirmations to help you swallow this principle more easily, but for now, envision this: to be please able is to allow his every effort; his every moment of even the slightest form of intimacy please you.

Affirmations of Please Ability

To heighten your please ability and thus change your man into the romantic, chivalrous lover you desire, say words of satisfaction out loud to him when he shows his sexual self. Here are some examples:

- That feels so nice.
- What a man.
- You are so awesome.
- I am so happy you are here.
- I love your touch.
- I enjoy your hugs.
- You are so strong.
- I love you.
- Thanks for this kiss.
- You make me feel so good.
- Raaarrrlll (cat call)
- You are 'all of that'!
- Do that again.
- I love it when you touch me like that.
- WOW, you look good!
- This is why I love you.
- Ha, ha, ha, ha.

- ❖ It is good you are mine.
- ❖ You are such a strong lover.
- ❖ Oh, YES!
- ❖ This is IT!
- ❖ You know how to really please me.
- ❖ I feel fantastic!
- ❖ WOW!
- ❖ What an awesome night.
- ❖ I feel heavenly.
- ❖ Fantastic!

The list can go on and on; just open up that mouth and let it rip! Being please able means knowing how to show that you are intensely happy. We have all learned how to show intense anger and to use force. Now it is time to learn feminine magic in the form of demonstrating intense please ability. Being please able is easy because men will believe what you say when you use these affirmations. Hell, men believe prostitutes and strippers and will pay them to talk this way!

So what if he never heard you speak this way before. Once you begin using this new language on each sign of intimacy, believe me, he will believe you. Men become more and more romantic when they feel that they are accepted sexually. Using these affirmations, the strongest ones in response to the delightful things he does, and the more relaxed ones when you really do not like the particular stimulus as much, will train your man to give you what you want. The better you like what he is doing, the more you gush! He will always start to go for pleasing you in the ways that he gets the most verbose responses about, and he will always enjoy pleasing you because you allow him to succeed. The weaker comments of affection serve to temper him. He will begin to repeat the behaviors that elicit the best response and he will feel safe with you because no matter what you are pleased by him.

The study of Tantra taught me to be a please able lover. I never have to press my husband for sex anymore. All I do now is appreciate each moment that he gives me and as his confidence builds, he is drawn inward to me. There was a time when he was afraid to have sex with me because based on his performance, the next day I may have either an attitude or a smile. It was too big a risk for him. If I had an attitude the next day, he would know that he failed to please me. The smile was nice, but too short lived. It is as though he was always taking a test in the bed, and waiting for my response the next day was probably terrifying! So now that I give him a favorable response no matter what, he feels safer in approaching me. (Of course, none of this joy would have been possible had I not simultaneously worked out my own childhood drama. I worked on being please able and healing from past wounds at the same time. One completes the other.)

For the ladies who have men who want too much sex for your taste, this principle works as well. Men crave the physical expression of love making because they really desire the feeling of accomplishment that comes from pleasing a woman. The feeling of maleness comes along with conquest and victory. When you begin to become more please able by giving compliments and affirmation to your man whenever he is intimate with you, you open him to the inner knowing that sex or no sex, he is pleasing you. Give him more praise when you are getting the subtle intimacy you desire. Give him subtle acceptance even when he is being aggressive sexually.

All he wants to know is that he is your champion and so the demand for physical intimacy becomes less when he knows you respect his drive no matter what. It does not mean that he will not want sex at all, but some of the drive is due to his wanting to know that he can please you physically. Also, when you practice being please able, you increase your pleasure principle. Practicing being feminine and please able increases your libido by default! Soon, you will be the love kitten that he can appreciate and he will be the protective and sensitive man you love.

This practice requires great patience, but when a man feels that his woman is appreciative of his love in and out of the bedroom, lapping up every drop as if it is the most pleasing thing on Earth, then he will want to please her all the more. If that means less sex, he will oblige, if it means more sex, then he will step it up! You have to try this for yourself. As is the case with all the principles in this book, do not ever tell a man that you are trying a new technique on him. Just proceed with your secret motives. In this case, the secrecy is warranted and quite feminine.

A Final Note on Please Ability

The most expensive female escorts in the world know this secret and so they lavishly indulge their cohorts with appreciation and affection. Many of you have expressed a concern that your man will think you are being insincere if you become please able after so many years of being 'normal'. Well, I beg to differ. I find that men believe what they are told about themselves. In fact, many psychologists, including John Grey and Laura Schlesinger, say that a man's identity is all wrapped up in the woman's feeling toward him. He is waiting for you to give him more approval, more successes and more verbal confirmation of his greatness. When you do, he will really appreciate you, and the bond between you will grow immensely. He will open to wanting to do more and more to get this feeling of success and joy; it is utter delight for a man to be appreciated by a woman.

No matter how new it is or corny it sounds, they respect your words because for them, words are not easy. In fact, women are known to talk more than men do, and as babies learn to talk before boys. In general, women have a better grasp on the use of language for communication, in contrast to men being more skilled at using their bodies and prowess.

Because using elaborate, new words of affection and love are difficult for men, they believe you when you speak healing words to them. Since forming these types of words takes vast effort, they respect your command of it and your ability to share that gift; it feels like an honor for them. You have to give them what they need to get what you want. Have fun with your new, romantic, lover!

Process #4 – Please Able Bath

Purpose: To balance the sexual harmony between you and your mate.

Items Needed:
- ✓ Honey
- ✓ Bubble bath
- ✓ Cinnamon
- ✓ Oranges (slices or wedges)
- ✓ Yellow candle
- ✓ A quiet Friday night

Exercise:
1. Run a nice bath using bubble bath, cinnamon, and honey in the water. Light the yellow candle as you pray for your Creator to come and assist you in rebalancing your sexual energies.
2. Undress and pray before getting into the tub. Ask aloud for the balancing that is needed. If you need to cool off and give your husband space ask for that, if you need to heat up and be more aggressive for the love of

your mate, ask for that. Use specific words. You may start this way; "I prepare this bath as a way to redesign myself from the inside out. I ask that the creator aid me by _____" (in regards to your sex life with your mate).

3. Get into the bathtub and relax. You may listen to soft music, hum, sleep, or just find a way to relax yourself.

4. Once you are relaxed, start to talk about what you want. Talk about the way that you want to or need to be in your relationship in regards to sex. Visualize yourself being that way. Start to bring forth the feeling of how it would be to live in a way that rebalances your love life.

5. Imagine your man being all you desire him to be. Let these images bring positive feeling and emotions.

6. Once you are feeling great and creating a new reality with your tears, laughter, ecstasy, and so forth, wash your entire body with the cut oranges. You may also eat an orange or two, taste some honey and experience the joy of creating a life that you want.

7. If you are in need of a stronger libido, wash all of your body, especially your sexual parts with honey and oranges. If you want your mate to be more sexually interested in you, wash between your thighs, lavishly, with honey and as you do visualize your mate being very attracted to you. If you need to cool off and not be so aggressive for sex, just use the oranges, no honey in the body washing. The honey will attract, the oranges will purify.

8. Enjoy your private time. Begin to get comfortable with the idea of pampering yourself in this way.

9. Repeat on Fridays as needed until your relationship begins to reflect your positive thoughts.

♀ Change Your Man ♂

Chapter 4: Make Him Happily Responsible – Allow Him His Comfort

OK, this is a biggie. Most every woman I have ever spoken to about this has confirmed it. The most disgusting and aggravating thing in the world, is watching a grown man just sit and relax. Yes, a grown ass man just sitting down, napping or doing absolutely nothing is so frustrating and irritating to us that we just cannot control ourselves when it happens, right? I cannot think of anything that irritates women more than this.

I mean consider the fact that we multitask; we can talk on the phone, make dinner, help the kids with homework, and balance the checkbook all at one time. Now imagine doing all of these tasks while looking in at your husband or boyfriend sitting on the couch watching the game. Worse than that, imagine working hard all day in addition to the ways I mentioned knowing that your husband is out enjoying a game of golf or chillin' on the basketball court. Now do you feel the burn? Ouch, that hurts!

The thoughts that cross our minds are violent when we think of it. I used to catch my husband napping at midday and just seethe with anger. I just wanted to throw something at him, but usually we keep it mild, right ladies? We will simply mention a chore that has gone undone for years, or ask him bluntly why is he so damned tired all of the time. When what we are really asking is, "Why is it so damned easy for you to sit and take a break when I hardly feel it my right to do so?"

Like me, many women only chose a moment of rest when no one else is looking. We find the most opportune time to steal a few moments when all the work seems complete and things are generally in order. To the contrary, men seem to be able to nap, rest, or lounge in the midst of chaos. My goodness, they are actually OK with the dishes sitting in the sink, the kids running crazy, and the checkbooks unbalanced. Why is that?

There are many theories circulating, but I agree with John Grey: men are born knowing how to receive and women are born knowing how to give. Because of this, men can make time to receive rest and rejuvenation at will, while women are so caught up in giving that we feel guilty when we need a break. We refuse to sit down and relax unless we believe we truly deserve a break. Unfortunately, this does not serve us well. Men are born knowing how to receive, so they are here on Earth to learn to give. They really do desire to give, but with a giver right there in his midst, it becomes unnecessary for him to step up to the plate. We refuse to exercise our most challenging areas: receiving rest, receiving assistance, and receiving the self-care that we refuse ourselves repeatedly. Being a born giver, it is our charge in life to learn to receive. It is time to gain ground in these areas.

If we want our men to be responsible, and supportive of our personal needs, we actually have to decide that we are going to allow him comfort while at the same time taking this same comfort for ourselves. We have to take a hint from those lovely guys by making self-care more important than any task remaining on the to-do list; If not, we will never achieve our objective – his happiness and our own. Most importantly, he will never exercise his objective on Earth, which is to learn to give support happily and willingly. They are literally leaning to be responsive and responsible.

It should not hurt us to see him happy and relaxed; it only bothers us because we are not. Happiness and relaxation are choices that we make on a minute by-minute basis. If only we allowed him comfort and allowed ourselves the same, or even more, we could change our men into responsible, happy guys, which would create a happy home with happy us to enjoy it!

Comfort Control

For the first ten years of our marriage, my husband would often accuse me of exhibiting a form of direct confrontation called comfort control. Comfort control is a 'cute' way of summarizing the series of behaviors that unfold when women become resentful of a man getting his rest or taking a break. We attempt to control his comfort by giving a task or disturbing him in another way. Men young and old experience this phenomenon at the hands of mothers, wives, girl friends, and even their daughters.

The comfort-control technique is actually nothing more than a glitch in the system, or a simple misunderstanding between men and women, in general. Since, misunderstandings can lead to ugly little battles that sometimes end in divorce, it is imperative that I come clean about what this form of direct confrontation is all about.

Maybe you can learn from how I finally came to grips with my own comfort-control issues and embraced change. I was forced to look at the symptoms I exhibited and decided to change myself accordingly to achieve new results, so I promise you that this works. You can change too, but first you have to understand the symptoms and admit that you have a few of them.

Comfort Control Symptoms

Symptom #1 – Changing the Environment: My husband has always been an honest guy. For the first few years of marriage, he would never mention that I had this symptom. Simply stated, the symptom was that I would change the environment of his comfortable location or setting. Of course, I was aware that I was being a bitch when I did it, but I thought this was quite normal. No woman is happy when a man is pleasing himself, right? Soon after the seventh year, his tolerance for my foolishness ran short and he began to open up to me. He began to point out specific instances when I would disturb him while he was trying to relax. He would argue that whenever he would get into a truly comfortable place with lights, sounds and temperature just the way he liked, I would come and change something, interrupting his peace. He referenced changing the thermostat in the room where he slept, or turning on the ceiling fan or my turning the lights on that had been off for his comfort.

The first symptom is easy to recognize. If you are the type of woman who decides to inadvertently shift the environment when your man is sleeping by changing the lights, sounds, temperature, channel or settings in anyway, begin to notice that you are doing it. What you are saying by shifting a place of comfort that he created for himself is that you resent his rest and actually, you resent him for exhibiting self-care.

Symptom #2 – Injecting Chores to Interrupt Comfort: My man would accuse me of asking him to do household chores once he had settled in for a nap or to watch a game. He would sight times when I would set a weekend agenda that included him and his body with little regard to his grueling workweek. He would point out the anger he picked up in my aura when he was just taking a moment to himself, putting off the chores that I obsessed about, and grabbing some down time.

This symptom is also easy to recognize. If you decide to talk to your man, or even suggest to him the chores that are undone as he lounges on the couch, wakes from a nap, or decides he will spend the day golfing, you are exhibiting this comfort control symptom. What needs to happen is your becoming awake in the moment and realizing that this is a form of direct confrontation and that there are better ways to deal with situations such as these that will get you what you want, which is your own sense of self-love, relaxation and peace and for your man to take responsibility.

Symptom #3 – Causing Physical Pain During a Man's Comfort: My man actually accused me of inflicting physical pain on him when he is trying to relax! He recalled instances when I would pick a scab off his back or prick a facial hair in an aggressive, yet playful way, during his time on the couch. What? Yes, he claimed that even in my lighter moments, I had an objective to make sure he was feeling the bite of my stress and my own personal obsessions with constant perfection.

One of the most foolish examples of my alleged comfort-control issues is his rendition of the birth of our first son, when I bit the man's ear as our first son dove head first from my birth canal. Mind you, I do not recall biting his ear. Furthermore, I was having a home birth with no medicine, monitors or allopathic help. We had chosen to birth this way, and it was a beautiful birth, but I just cannot recall the moment that I injured my husband. He told me that the bite was hard and that it caught him at a very sensitive lobe location. He claimed I made sure he would not enjoy the moment of our first son's birth due to the stinging pain.

He claims that because I was working in the labor of the baby, while he stood aside to watch, that I was making him pay for relaxing. He understands that I was in pain, but he firmly believes that because I was going through the pain of labor, I had to include him just for the sake of evening the score. This, he claimed, was my way of making sure that he too was experiencing everything that I was. Why would I do this? Well, according to him, I do not want to see him happy, peaceful or relaxed while I am going through stress, fatigue or 'drama'.

This symptom may be a little more difficult to spot and not all women, obviously, have this. However, be circumspect and look at the times when you playfully pinch or hit your man, look at the ways you tussle with him and then examine your motives. Are you picking a secret fight by joking with him in ways that might be considered painful? Do you play these love games during his time of rest? I found that maybe there was some truth to his accusations, although farfetched.

Symptom #4 – Interrupting His Sleep: This one is so common that I do not even need to give an example from my experience. A sleeping man is the easiest target for comfort control. There are so many things that a woman can do to disturb her man's sleep. Many men have noted that women often shift and move in the bed if she is displeased that he is sleep and she is not. They claim we decide to read at night or get up from the bed or switch on the TV when we feel slighted as he sleeps and we cannot. This symptom may seem nitpicky but it is a real experience for men I have spoken to and they claim we do it intentionally although subconsciously.

Symptom #5 – Poo Pooing an Activity that Brings Him Comfort: My husband used to come to me prior to planning a weekend activity to make sure that I was OK with it. For instance, if he were going to go play golf, or enjoy an afternoon at Starbucks wrapped in a good book, he would ask me if it was OK. Soon, however, he noticed a pattern of my thwarting his plans by informing him of all the work that needed to be done, discouraging him by deeming the activity frivolous or simply deciding that I did not like the friends he was going to meet. He claims that this is the reason he stopped asking and began telling me what he was going to do. Rarely did I just accept his proposal and give my blessing. This is also an easy one to spot.

Symptom #6 – Blaming Him for the Discomfort of Your Experience Due to His Comfort: When he did go out and do his thing, he could expect hell to pay upon his arrival home. Of course, I would bitch and moan about his outing running down the list of all the things I had to take responsibility for in his absence. Rarely, he states, did I simply ask him how the day went or tell him that I was glad he had a break. Instead, I would make him feel guilty by expressing my own discomfort due to his departure. This stole the joy and pleasure of his self-care. Plus it made him feel less than successful.

If you exhibit this symptom, there are easy ways to remedy the situation. In my case, I was actually conscious of these complaints, but it was not until I decided to practice my own brand of self-care that I could actually be peaceful with him doing his thing.

Hidden Vendetta

How foolish he was to accuse me of trying to control his comfort, or so I thought. Now ladies, of course I did not accept this lunacy at first. I never meant to directly confront my mate by spoiling his comfort. I did not have a hidden vendetta against this lovely human being, and my best friend. I could not even consciously recall most of the instances that he spoke of. Wait, this is a clue! I could not consciously recall the incidents, so maybe his being kind enough to recognize that these occurrences were subconscious was the ticket to my being able to explore this without feeling judged. The idea that I had a subconscious motive felt better. I just did not understand why he would incriminate me and make up stories that just were not true. The entire notion seemed foolish that a grown woman would actually plot against her husband to launch unnerving attacks during his sleep!

Even with thoughts of anger, I began to study my own behavior. I simply began to meditate on the instances that he was talking about; being honest with myself, looking into things more deeply than I had ever before, I began to take this form of direct confrontation more seriously. I had to do this work to save my marriage. If I had a secret vendetta, I was going to find it and root it out all together.

Getting Real for a Moment

In all fairness, a man getting comfortable in a house where the activity of the day included children running and screaming, food cooking, endless cleaning, load after load of laundry, money crunching, grocery shopping, chauffeuring children, homework helping and general project management that would make your head spin, felt a little insulting. I mean, sometimes his ability to just come in from a long day and RELAX became aggravating for good reason. It seemed unfair, somehow, that he could actually come home and lounge when I worked incessantly and endlessly all day long without feeling one iota better at the end of the day. By nightfall, I would feel the stress of my self-abusive habit of multitasking. His damned lounging was something that I could not even conceive of doing until I felt more accomplished and successful at what I was trying to do and be at home.

Never once did I view his ability to rest as a positive attribute; oh, to the contrary, I would pass his ability to rest off as laziness. In fact, the anger brewing within would compile upon itself attracting more thoughts. I would think of all the days I had found him being lazy, taking time out of his day to nurture himself with sleep. I would think of all the times I had been expected to do more than him. He seemed to get off easy in the world of managing our family and home.

In those years, my husband was working very hard as a technical consultant, but it seemed easy compared to what I was doing. I tried to compare being pregnant with a third while raising a 2-year-old and 4-year-old, to getting dressed each morning and hanging out in a plush office all day. The comparison seemed lopsided, Blackberry or baby bottle, board meetings or grocery shopping, changing diapers or changing screensavers, which is better? I simply could not find the relative balance among the two. I felt as though my job as mother was just far more difficult. I had never been in a corporate environment and so it was easy to for me to assume.

So when he laid his head to rest at night, especially if it was prior to my even having a thought to rest, I fumed, and my mind would fill with wild thoughts of anger, and sometimes even rage. Maybe turning on a bright light in the room we shared, or making some annoying noises would pay him back for his inconsiderate retirement. Of course, I never equated this with being confrontational. I was simply having dramatic, emotional responses to his arrogance. His arrogance was the catalyst, not my own inability to find comfort and choose rest the way he could, right?

Wow, this was a trip! I was actually blaming him for my inability to rest. It never occurred to me that sitting on the couch next to him was an option. I actually love football, but something in me would urge me to stick to my guns. How dare he watch the game? The lawn was growing, the house was a mess, or I needed him to help with the children. These were all the usual rants I contemplated as to why he should not rest; the sheer drama was addictive. I could not help but continue with the argumentative behaviors and I would toss in some role reversal stuff in the mix, as well. I would exude that I would do it all myself, then complain out the side of my neck that I always had to cover all of the work alone.

Once I woke up to my own thoughts, both the old program and the new began to play in my head at the same time. While I might be thinking about how angry I was that he was resting, I also thought about the fact that I too could rest anytime I chose to. Once I began to think this way, it was almost game over for this comfort control problem. This pervasive form of direct confrontation was on its way out of my marriage and out of my psyche.

I began to know that once I changed the need to control his comfort and instead focused on creating more comfort for myself, putting off the demanding work I thought I had to do, he would become more responsible. There are logical reasons as to why allowing him his comfort creates more support from your man: a) if you would not try to manage every aspect of your home and chores, less would get done and he would feel more inclined to help out; and b) when you take better care of yourself, your man learns to take care of you responsibly. This is what I really wanted.

As I pulled back from comfort-control tactics, I began to have an internal discussion about what I actually wanted from my husband. I had long since decided that I did not want to be right about this. I had crossed 'Petty Pond' and was now walking down Womanhood Way. I was willing to admit that my behavior and his, for that matter, was not going to work. I had to get to the root of why I was so angry, stressed and unsettled all of the time. I wanted him to help me out, but I did not want him to do it unhappily. So in essence, I was forced to create this next principle.

Principle #4: Adopt Your Man's Ability to Create Comfort and He Will Adopt Your Ability to Take Care of Responsibilities

Admitting that none of it was his fault was the first step. It just was not his fault that things were so rough for me. In fact,

I found that I had blamed my husband for most all of my discomfort in life. What I actually wanted was quite simple; I wanted him to help me in the house when he walked in the door instead of just taking a break. I wanted him to understand each evening that after putting the children to bed, cleaning the pots, and multitasking all day long that I wanted him take over and provide loving support to me. I wanted him to help me rest the way he was able to rest. I wanted him to invite me to rest, give me permission to rest, and tell me that I did not have to do all of that and that I was not responsible for everything. I also wanted – as many women do – him to want to treat me to all the luxuries that I deserved based on my suffering in the home all day. Again, I had to admit that even though he was not doing these things, it just was not his fault. I create my life; I created this too!

I had to begin to appreciate my husband's ability to create the kind of comfort that eased his soul. It is a natural talent that men have that goes undervalued. We ladies have our own talents that are not seen as attributes by our men. But this is clearly where the buck stops. It is time to go ahead and be the bigger person and actually begin to see his ability to rest when he needs rest as a talent. When we can appreciate our men for this talent, we can more easily begin to accept that this is important and valuable. So valuable, that we too should try to incorporate this ability to relax and receive. Once we do, our men will see that we are pulling away from obsessive behaviors. They will begin to adopt the ability to handle more and more responsibilities. Expressing what we want is a part of that shift. The first steps are the most tedious. I had to begin to express to my husband what I wanted and needed and that I too wanted time to relax, and most importantly, that I wanted his help with all of this.

Steps Toward Change

Soon I decided to stop controlling his comfort and begin telling him what I wanted in ways that did not disturb him. When I considered telling him what I wanted, I found it funny and odd that I had never actually done so before in ways that would foster positive responses. I chose the perfect moments – careful not to disturb his peace – and began to share what I wanted using 'I want' statements, i.e.:

- ❖ I want to relax.
- ❖ I want to be invited to relax.
- ❖ I want help with the children.
- ❖ I want intimate time in the evening.

I was careful not to use any statement that included his name. And I was always mindful to ask him for advice on these issues rather than making demands. I had to stop making it his fault that I did not take the time to relax. I was careful not to make demands by adding the word 'you'. If I had said, "I want you to invite me to relax," I would have been making a demand. I had read enough books on love and men to know that demands do not cut it, even if made in a soft and loving voice. Because he did not feel indicted by my 'I want' statements (thanks to Laura Doyle, The Surrendered Wife), he felt comfortable enough to open up to me.

My husband began to share with me the times that he has tried to do these things. He expressed that when he did offer to help me (without my nagging him to help, which he always ignored) I would always turn him down. When he told me to stop working so hard, I likened his comments to that of an oath with no concept or clue about how to run a home. When he offered to help with the kids, I responded in negative ways that inherently questioned his ability to raise the children or conduct them with any sense of correctness. I used his invitations to sit on the couch with him as ammunition to prove his laziness and stupidity. Not to mention, I turned down his every request for me to sit and relax, especially when I felt the time was 'inappropriate'.

When he had asked me to take breaks, get a babysitter, relax and enjoy being home during the day, I scoffed at his comments as though he was making a mockery of my important tasks and treating our children like cattle. At night when he did used to stay awake and wait for me to come to bed, the extent of my pillow talk was lengthy discussion on the stresses of my day. I was always in a complaining mode. He would listen, but feel saddened by my unhappiness. When he offered suggestions or advice during that pillow talk, it set me off and made me defensive. It felt as though he was belittling me, micromanaging my life. I would only get more defensive each time he tried to advise me; little did I know it was due to my unwillingness to release control or allow myself to be cared for by him.

It all boils down to this: yes, as a young mother I wanted everything in the house to be perfect because I was seeking control. Because my husband was not seeking control through an obsession with having things appear pristine at home, I deemed him disgusting and shiftless. I was so self-righteous that I had actually cut off his desire to take responsibility. Because I refused to heed most of his suggestions, he decided to relax even more. He was not going to fight me to make me realize the error in my ways. He would just sit and receive all the ill-slated gifts of a perfect home that I offered and ensured based on my compulsive work ethics.

The Essence of the Comfort-Control Issues

My violent outbursts of comfort control were fetal attempts to even the score. I refused his advice to 'just relax', yet I did not want him to be happy while I was not. Misery loves company. Soon I began to piece this together like a puzzle. I used meditations and the very processes that I suggest to you in this book to unravel the issues. I asked the Universe to help me because I did not have time or money to go to counseling. I began to discover through my spiritual work that I was controlling because I had to keep up to a standard of excellence that was impossible to reach, especially without balanced leadership. I had become my own leader by rejecting my husband's ability to lead, so consequently, I was on my own appearing to be the only responsible party. Being on my own and isolated, I began to resent him because he was not in his role as leader and protector, and that was simply because I would not allow it.

The more I did, the less he did. The more I struggled, the more he had to recluse to drown out the stress he probably felt by not being allowed to help me. The more I complained the more useless and helpless he felt. His going into the cave of 'rest' was just retreat from being accessory to a failing family. Instead of admitting defeat, he decided to sleep it away, bathe the pain with the TV and just unplug from certain tasks. I refused to motivate his responsibility by accepting his ideas and follow his guidance, and I refused to allow him peaceful defeat and retreat.

He was not the leader of his home, he was a little boy – I was treating him as a son. I was attempting to be the perfect mother without accepting that the perfect mother is the core to a family structure that has a powerful leader. Without this leadership, my role would be impossible anyway. It is like yin being an impossible notion without yang. It was my job to accept his yang. Failed attempts on his part caused what I perceived as his laziness. Comfort control was the only course of action that made sense. If he were not going to take responsibility for our home and family, instead choosing to rest and relax – I became upset that he was so cozy and attempted to shut down his comfort.

Again, I had to look at the importance of my role as a woman, which was not a part of the course material for the 18 years I had attended prep schools and University. Opening up to him about how I felt and what I needed was hard enough, but actually taking his advice would have made me too vulnerable. To submit to his will on the way things should run in the family would have been the most difficult thing in the world. To go to him as an underdog having lost my battle against fatigue, admitting that I was not as great a project manager as I pretended to be, and asking for his leadership and guidance with a willingness to follow, was just not something I could do at that time.

Looking back, I know that I wanted his signed, sealed permission to sit down and I wanted his coaching. There was wisdom in the way he did things and he never seemed stressed or burdened with chores. Sure it was easy to call him lazy and just detached from the household duties...there was wisdom in the way he regulated himself. I wanted support and management from him, but asking for that seemed to have been admitting failure, or emotional inadequacy. To take the ultimate step and heed his advice as though he was my manager felt like losing my identity; a death of sorts that I was just not prepared to handle.

So I had found the source of my comfort control issues, but how could I exorcise this behavior from my life? On top of the fact that I was not doing the best job caring for myself, I was ineffective in attempting to manage his self-care. Even as I discovered these truths, I continued to take each opportunity to castigate him when I worked and he rested. Even as I was in a state of transition and meditation on the matter, I had to stay safe in my old persona. I was so self-righteous that I did not even see the final lesson of this exploration until late in the game.

Comfort Control Interrupts Intimacy

As I grappled with this pattern and began to unwind the root to my need to control and interrupt his comfort, I began to have an even deeper realization. When it was all said and done, his emotional and intimate needs had gone unmet for several years. Discussions about his day at the office were virtually non-existent. I never even checked in with him to find out if there was anything I could do for him – I mean especially for him – like a massage, intimate time, washing his hair, feeding him his favorite foods, complimenting him, cherishing him with lavish actions, or just being available to listen to him. These items were just not on my long to do list. No wonder he found so much time for his own self-care. He had to use the TV to entertain himself because I was not very entertaining. Of course, he had to get nurtured by taking long naps; I was not providing anything that might get his mind off of work and into a peaceful state. Come to think of it, depressed people sleep and drown their sorrows in TV and other distractions. Could our men be depressed about their own failure to be happy and responsible in our homes? Of course they are!

My work was piling up. Not only would I have to rewire my subconscious to stop the comfort-control tactics, I would also have to begin to take his advice, which meant submitting to his will. I would have to begin to give our marriage the same respect that I gave everything else on my to-do list, but in a more relaxed and easy way. I would have to learn to relax and take his advice. I would be a student. This was indeed scary.

I had to be patient with myself, but by using the processes I have designed, I did it! I slowly changed my behaviors and when I did, I saw my husband become responsible and happy. He spent more time than ever before in our home helping me to be happier and have more time for self-care. When he suggested I take a break while he kept the children, I simply left the house. No need for making lists and notes on how to care for the children, I decided to trust him.

When he suggested that I sit for a moment with him and chill, I did it! I simply released the thought of all that needed to be done and I followed his advice. When he decided to go to play golf on a Saturday, I got a baby sitter and went to enjoy myself as well. He had always wanted me to have activities that suited my personality and interests. Also based on his recommendation, I hired a housekeeper to help with all the chores, which helped immensely. All it took was my stepping back and allowing him to lead.

You too can make your man responsible by noting some of the very things about yourself that I explained. Once your home is a bit more stable, and you are practicing self-care and following your husband's advice on the matter, it might be helpful to add the practice of Feng Shui to your bag of feminine tricks. I learned how to heighten my own comfort and his by using the ancient art of Feng Shui. Here is the process. Try it for yourself.

Process #5 – Feng Shui

Because the work of releasing control of home and practicing self-care is so difficult for many women, I will share a great fix. Learn the art of Feng Shui! Feng Shui is an ancient Asian and African art to creating peaceful environments in the home. Adding Feng Shui to your skill set can help you energize your home. I was able to create a peaceful environment conducive to my own relaxation, while doing something spiritual and positive for the entire family. You will enjoy creating your own peaceful spaces for relaxation in your home.

Feng Shui is the art of placement. Not only can you use these basic tips to create sacred spaces for your relaxation, but this process will also balance the energy in your home and encourage the man in your life to more easily get into the idea of taking responsibility for the family. A few simple steps will allow you to make your home and relationship into a wonderful environment of bliss. Increase your love and his buy-in by making these basic changes:

1. Remove all clutter from closets and donate old items you do not use.
2. Make the bedroom a haven; decorate with favorite colors and fabrics.
3. Place pictures of joy around your house; couples, children and scenery. Place pictures of men being manly and women relaxed.
4. Keep toilet seats closed at all times when not in use.
5. Place a running fountain in your home.
6. Use creative colors to paint your walls.
7. Study gemstones and place them strategically in the home for energy.
8. Purchase all the things needed for peaceful baths; take one bath per week.

For more Feng Shui tips, stop by your nearest library and pick up a book on the method. I like the Black Hat School of Feng Shui rather than the Compass School. Feng Shui can aid you in building your own comfort.

Recommended Feng Shui Books:

❖ Feng Shui Made Easy, William Spear, 1995. Harper SanFrancisco
❖ Feng Shui For The Home, Evelyn Lip, 1984. Heian International

♀ Change Your Man ♂

Chapter 5: Make Him Successful – Be his Biggest, Corniest Cheerleader

Do you want your man to become more confident and self-assured? All women like successful men; you know the ones who achieve fame, fortune and public recognition. I call it the Barack Obama effect. All women love Barack, and even those who do not agree with his stances are admitted to being attracted to his energy. He is confident and self-assured. We like that, right ladies? He seems to be the type of upstanding man who would protect a woman, make her feel like a queen and not demand too much coddling based on insecurity and fear.

We all love confident men, so why not make your man confident and self-assured like Barack? It is so easy to do. To change a man into a confident person, all you have to do is cheer him on. Men derive so much of their personal self-image based on the ways he is viewed by the women he loves. His mother, sisters and especially his mate can actually shift his confidence to ultra max simply by catering to his ego.

Ladies, do not lose me here. It may seem unfair that we have to cater to a man's ego in order to make him confident, but think of it this way, catering can also be viewed as nurturing. When we boost our children's self-image with positive talk and compliments, cheering each new step they take, we do not think of it as 'catering to the ego'. But it works for them and they grow in esteem with our nurturing. In like manner, we must nurture our men in order to grow them to the point where they become self-confident. Is it our job to make this happen? Well, yes and no. The real question is, "Do we want a confident, successful man or not?" If the answer is yes, then of course it is our job to put in work toward this end. All we have to do is affirm him, enjoy him, compliment him

153

when he does well, and appreciate him publicly and privately. Maybe your man already walks with a swagger and is comfortable asserting himself. If you feel your man is already quite self-assured, then skip this chapter and move on to Chapter 6...lol.

It is so easy to cheer him on. This is about simple respect for your man, the same respect you want from him. Often we are not trained in this subtle feminine art. We are more skilled at finding a fault, which goes back to our educational background. In what classroom was it that we learned to find what is right about a given situation? Instead, we were taught to find what is wrong.

Do you recall the magazine Highlights and the picture with the hidden items that had the caption 'What is Wrong with this Picture'? We were trained from kindergarten to find the problems and pounce! But if we had been trained by wise women in the ways of real womanhood, we would know that it is much more valuable a skill to learn to find the good qualities in life and praise them. For when we do, the self-fulfilling prophesy kicks in – what we believe about a person shapes that person's belief about himself and the actions he will be most prone to take. Because we are taught the ways of confronting problems, we inadvertently use this psychology on our men.

If you directly confront your man in public or private pointing out his faults in vivid and loud ways, you will pay the price in the long run, as he will be unlikely to behave in ways that exude confidence. On the other hand, if you choose to compliment your man abundantly and lovingly in public and in private, he will respond by living up to your expectations and beliefs about him. It is best to nip insults in the bud and replace them with loving, engendering positive talk. This will draw your man in and endear him to you, his greatest support, and at the same time make him into the confident and successful stud you always dreamed of.

Nipping Insults in the Bud

Some women argue that it just does not matter, and the insults and jokes should not make a difference. After all, if the man is defective, we have to point out the problems in order to solve them, right? Wrong, wrong, wrong! Pointing out the problems, and especially in a joking manner, will only exacerbate the issues. Many women, however, thrive on using humor and lighthearted put downs to relate to men. Because we never learned the art of feminine flow, we use our more developed parts of humor and wit to communicate our issues with our men. The women who thrive in this energy will likely conclude that men need to lighten up and let go of the ego, why not learn to laugh? Furthermore, witty women conclude that telling a story about a person, especially a funny story, should not have drastic results or cause emotional damage, even if the story does point out his very real flaws.

I challenge these women to put themselves in the man's shoes. Try to imagine what it would be like to be a man, a species who actually thrives on being seen by the world as a success, and be publicly or privately called on his 'stuff" in ways that demean or offend him. It probably hurts like hell. If you do not believe that the male species is inclined to want success, be victorious and be revered and respected both publicly and privately, then you must read John Grey's book Men are from Mars and Women are from Venus. He talks extensively about the male need to feel special, successful and valued. Women too have this need but to a lesser extent. More important for women is the need to feel loved, honored and secured.

So to nip these public insults in the bud means to understand the ways that they devastate a relationship. Here is a list of the negative effects of joking or insulting your man in public or private:

- ❖ Men become sullen and listless.
- ❖ Men feel like a failure.
- ❖ Men feel develop a strong vendetta against woman.
- ❖ Men feel a sense of guilt that he is not performing.
- ❖ Men become unable to share intimate space with the woman.
- ❖ Men lose trust in the women.
- ❖ Men feel as though the women are not supportive of him.
- ❖ Men feel a sense of isolation from the woman.
- ❖ Men begin to do passive aggressive things to return the favor.
- ❖ Men live up to the insinuated negative expectations of the woman.
- ❖ Men begin to detach from the woman.
- ❖ Men begin looking for women who will honor him.
- ❖ Men become more likely to cheat on the woman.
- ❖ Men decide that he must prove himself.
- ❖ Men lose hope in future successes.

Two Examples of Men and Their Wives

The effects of joking and insulting your man publically and privately are severe. The above chart lists some of the possible fallouts involved in this sort of treatment. Some of you may be looking as though you still do not understand the recklessness in making a joke or two every now and again. What you do not realize is that you are actually throwing a punch with words. You may recoil into the notion that men should be able to take this treatment seeing as they are so strong and self-sufficient. However, these conclusions are not based on fact. Read the two examples below of generic men and their wives. You will begin to feel the difference between supporting and thwarting a man with your words.

Imagine you are **Generic Man #1**. You are in public with your loving wife. Maybe out at dinner, or even at a public event. Friends and family are gathered and the conversations range from boring to bravado. Each member of the party listens to the other for entertainment and connection. The social circle is enhanced by great food and wine.

Your lovely wife, **Generic Wife #1** is opening a conversation about you. Uh oh, you have been here before. What is she going to say? You review your last week together, had you made a funny mistake, had she found you on the floor with the kids playing with what you thought was Play-Doh, but was actually green slime that stuck to the carpet? Had you fallen from a ladder or ordered the wrong paint color? Or would it be the one about Las Vegas when you won $1,000 at poker and then gambled it away at the roulette table? What stories would you cringe at and how would you defend yourself against her reckless joking? You want to be perceived as a winner, of course, but she thinks you are a loser and here she is about to speak on it.

So she opens her mouth to speak, oh man, she is telling the one about the day you took off from work thinking it was Presidents Day and how your boss had called frantic to find you as you lay around in your boxers and had a late lunch of burgers and fries? Your wife is actually sharing the story as though it is funny exchanging knowing looks with the other women at the table. But the men are there too. The men who now know that on your off days you do not even get dressed until noon and that instead of playing golf or exercising like a respectable man, you indulge in burgers and fries – now they view you as a college freshman type. How would that affect your status among them? How would you defend yourself? You had actually made the terrible mistake that she jokes about and you are still paying the makeup game at work to cover your tracks. How sad.

Would this sort of 'humor' endear you to the person making the jokes? You would probably just laugh it off – better to laugh than to cry. But you would probably begin to either give up on receiving the type of reverence that any working, striving, devoted and loving man deserves or you would begin to move into the cave and away from this open dismissal of your manhood. It depends on your background. Unfortunately, you saw your dad go through this with your mom, so you know all too well the feeling of rejection and dismissal involved. You never thought you would become like your dad, but here you are demeaned and abused. Why did you marry her? Dear God!

Women, all too often, do not even know that through this public or private joking, she alienates the very man who depends upon her most for support. We have not been 'schooled' to know that a man's partner is even closer than his mother is. He is depending on her to present something new about him. He knows his faults, so now he needs to know his attributes.

Now imagine **Generic Man #2** in public with his wife. This man is not nervous about what his wife will say at the business dinner, the family dinner, or even without him amongst her girlfriends. **Generic Wife #2** is in the good habit of observing the conversations of others and injecting engaging stories about her man's successes, while making it a point to smile and share his better qualities in such a way that does not seem to boast, but inspires other wives to find the hero is her husband.

Oh sure, **Generic Wife #2** has silently poked humor at her husband and has even had ample cause to revert to teasing him, but she rarely takes advantage of the opportunities. Rather, she consciously decides to become her husband's tasteful and elegant cheerleader. Unlike Generic Husband #1, her husband seems proud of his accomplishments and glad that he has a woman by his side supporting him. In fact, **Generic Wife #2** gets invited way more often to company events, picnics and outings than **Generic Wife #1** (who of course complains about feeling left out...lol) He grins and feels the heat of passion swell as his wife acknowledges his better qualities in public. He especially loves it when she tells his own parents what a great husband he is and how much she loves him. In a way, this completes the circle of his growth allowing him to experience the approval and validation that grown men, and indeed the human species, need to live a decent and respectable life.

Which husband feels more endeared to his wife, **Generic Husband #1**, who is secretly resentful or maybe just wistfully unmindful of his wife making a public mockery of him, or is it **Generic Husband #2** who is being portrayed as a hero in circumstances that uplift him in front of the world? Would you be most satisfied with the wife who treats you like an absolute super hero in public and in private or the one who degrades you with jokes that she does not even ask your permission to tell?

Principle #5: Treat Him Like an Absolute King in Public and in Private

So this principle is simple. We are talking about basic respect, kindness, and human dignity. It is very important that you do not laugh this chapter off, but see the real duty we have as women to posture ourselves in such a way as to allow our men to be seen as a hero through our eyes. It is important to note that a man is always in search of his success. With all of his heart and soul, he wants to know that he is doing the right things and is succeeding in life and in love.

I would like to share a brief story with you - you know me and my stories. Recently my husband took a brief business trip on a weekend to Washington, DC. I became suspicious of him wondering who works on weekends in DC. My insecurity made the weekend conversations tense. But once he returned home, he told me the truth. He had gone to DC on the weekend to see an old friend of ours. She is not a love interest, rather, a close friend of his. He told me that he loves her company because she compliments him. She tells him specifically that he is a good man. She admires him as a husband and father and showers him with loving words of his accomplishments, framing him as successful, admirable and honorable.

He loves her company so much that he forfeited a weekend with his family to leave earlier for a business trip to DC to spend time with her. I was so grateful that he shared his real reason for leaving two days early for a Monday business trip, and I was so proud of myself for accepting the importance of his interaction with her. Sure, I felt a little slighted by the fact that he had not shared this in the beginning, but he told me he was afraid of my reactions. He did not want me to ruin his chances to be in her presence. In order not to risk my shutting his plans down, he went ahead without my knowledge and consent.

This should clearly demonstrate the importance of Principle #5. Men prefer being treated like a king. It is not unfair or unwarranted. We ladies enjoy being treated like a queen so of course its reciprocal would be the case. Let's do it! But first let's make sure that we are not doing the other naughty things that would degrade our men and force them into getting this need met elsewhere.

How Do You Know You Are DOING IT?

Due to the natural honor system that men seem to adopt in this culture, women are oftentimes more guilty of this behavior than men are. Women will insult men in public using this witty format in many ways. Here are some examples that might help you pinpoint your own foolishness. Do you:

- Talk about the fact that he gets lost on the road?
- Imply that his income is too low?
- Insinuate that he plays the lottery, gambles or cheats on taxes?
- Share the fact that he leaves his clothing on the floor or is messy?
- Suggest that he does not complete his chores?
- Comment on his looks, smell, or attitude?
- Imply that he is a pitiful excuse of a man?

I could go on, but what would be the point? I would rather get to the important business of solving this dilemma. For some women, there is a sense of power derived from telling bad news about our men in public. It may seem funny to us, but at the root of the issue, there lies a need to appear 'better', more sane, rational, reasonable, and responsible than he does. Maybe we feel superior to him and want to share that news with the world to make ourselves feel better. After all, he does not really appreciate us, so a good public laugh at his expense will reduce his ego a few notches, besides he does not mind this sort of joking anyway, right? We may thinks it is cute and funny, but believe me ladies; he does not think it is cute at all. His laughter at these remarks sure up his ego. Nevertheless, the deep, sustained hurt is difficult to deflect.

Self-Test

The easiest way to diagnose the problem is to invite a group of familiar friends to dinner. Pay close attention to the conversations. Try to watch yourself from the inside. Realize moments in which you would usually inject a funny thing about your mate just for laughs. As well, try to include some praise of your husband in front of your guests and note the level of resistance you feel in your body to publicly praising him. If there is no resistance, just praise him and watch how his body language is affected. Here are some ideas in terms of how to praise a man publicly:

- ❖ My husband is so awesome; let me share a story…
- ❖ My man takes such good care of me; let me tell you what he did…
- ❖ I love being in this relationship; he is so kind.
- ❖ This is the most fun I have had in years; my husband is hilarious!
- ❖ He keeps me laughing!
- ❖ You should see the project he completed this weekend…
- ❖ My husband is great with the kids…
- ❖ I am so proud of him; let me share what he did…
- ❖ I was so happy when he _____, he is really good at it!

These are just a few examples of cheerleading for your man. I realized early on that whenever I tried to lift my man up with my words in public that it seemed difficult. It felt like a cat had my tongue and the thoughts could not come clearly. I started to keep track of the number of times that I complained about my man to my friends in public versus the times I bragged about what a stud he is, or how he had fixed the garage door opener, or that he was just the sweetest man on the face of the planet…the results were scary. It appeared that I had a much harder time complimenting my man in public. I felt more powerful, witty and hip when I got the crowd to laugh at something that he was failing at. Such a sad wakeup call!

Publicly insulting your man is a covert form of direct confrontation. A direct confrontation does not have to be in the form of verbally yelling or cursing. This covert way of putting him down and asserting actual superiority must end at once. Once you diagnose the issues and feel where you are on the scale, begin to weave public and private compliments of him into your daily operations

A Final Example

I know a woman who used to tell what she thought was a funny story about her husband; I thought it was mean. Nonetheless, we heard the story so many times in our youth that we committed it to memory and would lip synch the words whenever she retold it. The story was about her and her husband walking with their baby at an open park. Suddenly, she looked up to find daddy and baby had disappeared! Apparently, dad had fallen into a hole as deep as a man with the baby in his arms! She tells it as if this father, being shiftless and clumsy, was walking without thinking, and had failed to secure the infant. She insinuates that he was so careless that he must not have seen this gigantic hole.

Each time she recounts this rather belittling story, usually in large groups of friends, she rolls with laughter making sure to point out the fact that he never pays attention to anything and to be so careless with the baby – how crazy was that! I watched her husband's face as this story was told. He would always attempt to laugh with us, but sometimes it just seemed so contrived. I could tell how hurt he was on the inside and how much anger he stored on his wife. This woman had no idea what she was doing to the relationship. With each telling of this and other such stories, it was obvious that he was taking steps away from his wife and from the children as well. Why not step up and defend himself? Was he being humble? The funny thing about the male ego is that for men, it seems they have an easier time pulling away into a safe cave of isolation rather than directly confronting us, and rightfully so!

I saw this happen as a young person and instantly recognized the game. In my young mind, I made up a counter game that may help couples with in this scenario. It is called Daily Play. This is practice for women who want to endear their husbands to them, as well as play their role in creating a successfully, confident man.

Process #6 – Daily Play

Purpose: To practice the habit of daily lifting your man's spirits.

Items Needed:
- ✓ A note book
- ✓ A good attitude

Exercise:

Week #1 – Grab your notebook and prepare to list daily all the things you like about your man.

Begin with listing the simple character traits you love about your man. As the days pass, go beyond the basics to find the little things he has done for you that you appreciate.

Write short stories about the really great times you have shared together. Jot these memories in your notebook daily for one full week.

End of Week #1 – You should have seven pages of wonderful things about your man; great stories about his chivalry and kindness, even stories of how he has protected and cared for you in the all the ways you love.

Week #2 – Now is the time for practice...practice sharing these compliments, stories and short loving words out loud in front of a mirror. Alone and in front of a mirror you can let the words come out of your mouth freely. Have fun with this practice phase so that when you step into the reality of actually saying these things to him, the words will feel comfortable. It is similar to memorizing lines for a play except this performance is going to affect your marriage in really profound ways.

Practice as many times as you need to. Prepare yourself well by using the many examples in your notebook. Make cute antecedents about your guy. Isn't this fun? Go ahead and laugh at yourself practicing making nice to your man! It's funny, right?

Another way to practice is by using light meditation. As you lie in bed at night, envision yourself saying these lovely compliments at parties, in private with your guy, in front of the children and to your parents with your guy watching. This will really prepare your mind to act.

End of Week #2 – You should have a level of comfort with visualizing all the times and ways you might utter sweet nothings about your guy. You have filled your mind with ideas, and believe me your spirit will do the rest. Do not be so rigid that you get tense. Let this flow easily. The practice is just a symbol to the Universe that you are going to implement some new behaviors. It is not a test and it is not pass/fail. If you need another week to practice, give yourself that luxury. You have all the time in the world.

Week #3 – This is the time for the actual implementation of the new behavior. Now you are going to inject into your marriage this new form of loving communication, and the results will dazzle you! You have written clear examples of your husband's goodness and love. You have practiced complimenting him in the mirror and in your mind.

Now is the time to begin inserting these little compliments into your conversation. You should try to inject one on the first day of the week and then build to two the next day and so forth. Build this practice until you average communicating at least five compliments daily.

Do not reserve all of your complimenting for the private moments you share with your man. Be sure to brag to your friends, family and children about how fabulous your man really is. Tell them all the details of his fabulousness. Include stories of all the times he has done things that feel good to you. Be sure to share these with his parents. This will really bolster the fact that he is a success, something his parents have always wanted for him. And it is real! You are simply, for the first time giving public acknowledgement of him in a consistent way.

End of Week #3 – You will be delighted about your own success. You are using kindness to sure up your relationship. He will begin to see himself differently all because of you, and this will endear him to you. You will also be happy to know that you are putting loving energy into the Universe and what goes around comes around. Expect deeper intimacy and a heightened sense of bonding between you. Enjoy your newly confident man and watch as his glow broadens and makes him irresistible in every way. You are building into him the most important factor of a man's nature – success!

Enjoy and document the many blissful moments that occur. You may want to repeat the process once you have concluded round one making new notes about more, great complimentary offering to your husband. This can get really elaborate, and why not? Would you not want him to be as complimentary? Of course, you would. We always receive just what we give.

♀ Change Your Man ♂

PART TWO: Change Him for the Better – Stop Giving Directions

I know you have heard the ancient joke about a man being lost on a road trip, where instead of admitting that he is lost, he just continues on the journey with the willful knowledge that he will find his way without stopping for help. Since the female passenger is not allowed to tell him to stop for directions, she must gently wait for him to figure things out less she suffer the wrath of being labeled pushy.

Emphatically speaking, men hate being directed. This is not said as an insult to them, but instead because it is a fact. In general, men should not feel insulted by this parody, and most do not. They want us to see them as 'all knowing', and let's face it ladies, we love the all-knowing type. Secretly, we love a confident man who is eager to stand in his manhood and run the show. Just imagine the rapper, 50 Cent, who appears to be, at least externally, very masculine taking directions from a woman, hanging on her every word like a young boy and needing her help and direction in public to find his way around town.

Being directed, especially by a woman, goes against everything they believe about themselves. It simply offends a man to have a woman constantly directing him. The male ego is a powerful thing and easily becomes broken in a relationship where the woman wants to be the boss, even if he allows her to run the show.

It amuses me that women are often turned off by a very direct male energy. I happen to think strong, protective male energy is wonderful! Whatever happened to women loving men who are strong, confident and able? It is a sad state of affairs when women desire men who are more sensitive and open to being instructed. Usually women who want this type of man have had difficulty in relationships with direct and very 'manly' men. However, this difficulty is merely because of the training to be men they received in grade school. But to resort to a more gentle character is not always the solution.

A woman will easily become bored with a man whom she can shove around. Speaking for myself, secretly I wanted to be put into my place, and I am glad that I choose a man who demands my respect. I feel that my place of being protected and cared for as a woman is sacred and wonderful and I enjoy it immensely. Furthermore, I have come to know that almost every woman I have ever worked with feels the exact same way, although they would never admit it. To be vulnerable and in need of protection is not fashionable, I guess.

I have opened and shared my stories in this book to aid other women who seek to have better relationships with their mates. I admit that in the past, I was one of those women who wanted to control and direct my man by being in a position of power. This energy has backfired so many times causing my mate to retreat into a cave, leaving me isolated in our relationship. I have seen him recoil and go deep into mental seclusion by simply ignoring my directives and blatantly or passively going against what I said. In the end, the only way for a man to get his power back is to become passive aggressive. If the woman becomes the negative aggressor, he takes a passive-aggressive role. When the woman takes a positive-passive role, the man will take a positive-aggressive role.

When I refer to the term passive aggressive, I am talking about a man who is full of anger on the inside, but expresses it in a passive way so as not to openly confront his woman knowing she will actually enjoy a confrontation or fight. You see, my pseudo male really enjoyed his anger, which was a sign to me that my tactics were working and that I was getting him to understand me and hear me out. His anger was like a trophy to me, and probably too many of you who also use strong-armed tactics with your mates. Typically, after experiencing so much of my abuse, my husband knew that a head-on resistance to my bossing him would be futile. So instead, he took the protest underground.

He would do things like extend his workday or find activities to do that would keep him from family duties. He became more engrossed in TV and sports games, and he began to refrain from being in situations with me in which I had the worst record of giving unsolicited advice or directions, such as the mall, the grocery store, the kitchen, the house, with the children, at the in-laws', and the bedroom, basically everywhere!

Men truly want to be the hero, ladies, and deep inside, we want to be the beautiful princess that he rescues from the evil dragon. This is the true nature of men and women; natural orders that we have suppressed long enough. We have buried the primal need to live the truth of our genders deep in the subconscious mind in order to conform to this society's attempts to force everyone into a politically correct, impossible sameness. We come to devalue these primal needs and longings as gender-specific innateness becomes out of style for each of the sexes. Nevertheless, the urges to be in our traditional gender roles do seep back to the surface. And when we feel out of balance in our relationships, we do not know how to fix it, but we know how we want to feel. Men want to feel like the security and the king, and women want to feel secured and treated like a queen – usually.

The Making of a Female Dictator

This section discloses ways that women unwittingly become the dictator in relationships. It is important to note that falling into the pitfalls of directing our men is not entirely our fault, although it is our responsibility to recognize and shift it. I know it is because of the training in the modern school systems, the media and training from our parents that causes us to behave in a manner incongruent with our natural tendencies. The making of a dictator is simple, we are taught to strive to be right about most everything. Consequently, we want to be the one that our family comes to when in need of answers and such, husbands included.

We derive a sense of importance when the people around us come to us for advice, approval and assistance. The only issue with being in this sort of position is that we neglect our own personal needs and become martyrs in our relationships. We find ourselves weary of over mothering the people whom we refuse to wean. More importantly, in the case of our men, we begin to enable them by putting them in the position of coming to us for everything, which moves us away from our femininity and into the role of director. While directors are needed and revered, men need to feel as though they are the primary directors in the family. Moreover, if we are viewed as the person in our relationships with all the 'know how', we begin acting the part thereby rejecting our men when they try to take the wheel, if even for a moment, becoming excessive, hence, damaging the relationship.

Excessive Directing

Excessive directing comes in many forms. Although we want our men to be right sometimes, making him right is hard because it means we have to be wrong. My old belief is that he has to be wrong in order for us to be right; directing feels much better.

Another way we tend to direct is by trying to mold his style; if he is not going to be right, at least he can be cute. So we tell him what types of clothing to wear on vacation, out to dinner, and so forth. Seems like a load to handle, but we do it all in the name of micromanagement.

Additionally, women want to be cared for, though everyone knows that a leader provides a service. So if we have taken on the leadership position in our relationship, it is difficult to get serviced. Allowing him to care for us is something we have to relearn, and of course, the first step is stepping out of the leadership position.

In terms of his level of competence, we sometimes refuse to give him a chance to prove we can trust him. We actually compete for 'honcho status' so much that his competence does not get a chance to shine through.

Finally, we want our men to be accountable, right? We want him to commit to us in ways that leave us feeling secure in our relationships. This becomes almost impossible if we are the directors. By default, the one directing is in control of the partnership and determines the mission and vision of the relationship. So when we look to our man to account for a situation, he cannot show up if he is not in the directing position. When we remove ourselves from making all of the decisions, like magic they become more accountable over time.

♀ Change Your Man ♂

Chapter 6: Make Him Trustworthy – Trust Him

Trust is the single most important issue in the modern marriage, and begins with our connection to Source. Source is an easy concept; it is a filler word for what we might call God, i.e., Jehovah, Buddha, Christ, Allah, Obatala, Yahweh, and so forth. I use the word Source as a way for people of all traditions to understand the concept of Creator. Recently the movie, The Secret, rocked the planet. Everyone from Oprah to Good Morning America covered the topic of human beings creating a new reality using the power of thought. Quantum scientists the world over have explored this concept.

The basic theory is that our point of focus determines the outcome of any event. For instance, when we focus on the negative imaginings of all the ways our men might fail us, we attract the failure of our men. By mastering the Law of Attraction, we can have more success and more happiness in our relationship. The key factor in this is trust, which is the second step in the Law of Attraction. (We will discuss this in the next section.) We must decide to trust that Source will take care of us and fulfill our deepest needs.

Using the Law of Attraction is a process that requires focus and a willingness to change old ways of thinking. It is a process, which provides a great starting point to introducing the concept of trust. Whether we believe in the power of thought (Law of Attraction) or not, we all clearly understand the concept of trust or faith in a higher power. Making our men trustworthy requires that we have a quantum understanding of the importance of trust. Often, we ladies wait for our men to prove that we can trust them while the Law of Attraction advises a different order of events. In order to use the Law of Attraction we would have to decide to trust that Source itself will provide. But first we have to end the judgments, fears and doubts prior to our men changing in anyway. It is a concept that I have found altogether useful when it came to changing my man.

Once we have learned to trust that the Universe will provide all that we need and are in the habit of trusting that it is protecting us, then not only will we have learned to trust our men, but we will have learned to trust ourselves, our friends and all other persons in our environment as well. Once we begin to trust in these ways, our men will show up just as we expect them to as trustworthy beings. Our expectation of success in this area is enough to elicit from our men the behaviors we desire to feel safe and secure in our relationships. The successful use of the Law of Attraction is predicated upon us trusting the Universe to protect us, thereby expecting that our men are trustworthy right from the beginning. After all, would a loving and protective Source bring us anything less?

I have found that the successful implementation of the Law of Attraction has increased my ability to trust my man. Patience is required, but in taking this exercise to heart, we also gain the greater talent of the ability to trust Source. What a great way to live life! In learning to use the step-by-step application of this popular concept, I learned to trust that I am always cared for by a loving intelligence. This is bliss ladies, sheer bliss! The added perk was the fact that as I began to trust, I was able to let go of the need to control, because I was able to see that I had nothing to fear. I opened to the notion that all my needs, desires and cravings for safe haven in my home were answered. I shaped my man into a trustworthy being by simply deciding to trust not only him, but also the Universe itself to protect me in every conceivable way.

Step-By-Step Law of Attraction

The Law of Attraction has four steps:

Step #1 – We ask. We are to place our requests to the Universe as though ordering from a huge menu of possibilities. We can have all that we desire. All we have to do is ask our loving and intelligent Source.

Step #2 – We must trust. Trust simply means that we develop a strong inner knowing that the Universe will deliver on our requests. Trust is synonymous with and requires a huge amount of faith. We have to have faith that the Universe will deliver.

Step #3 – We have to allow. We have to allow ourselves to open to receiving the things that we are asking for. The largest part of allowing is feeling good. When we trust the Universe, we begin to feel good. By feeling good, we allow the things that we desire to flow into our realities. As long as we lack trust, we feel afraid. Feeling afraid brings into our realities more situations to be fearful about.

Step #4 – Finally, we receive. Receiving is the action step. It simply means that we act on the opportunities that are presented as ways to accomplish the very things we have asked for. Receiving also entails becoming more grateful for all that happens, knowing that the Universe is always delivering as promised. In this way, we begin to appreciate all experiences no matter whether they are good or bad. We receive the gifts of any situation and find the ways that the Universe is bringing us bounty!

The Most Challenging Step – Trust

This may seem like a really deep process, but on the contrary it is truly quite simple. Most women have the first step down pat; we know what we want and usually not only do we ask, we demand it of our men. A great way to avoid the demands is to ask Source rather than our men for what we want...to do this we simply pray, journal or meditate on what we truly desire.

The most challenging step for many of us is to trust. Once we ask for or demand what we want, the next step is to trust that it will happen. How does it look to us to trust a man to deliver all that we need? You are probably thinking, yeah right! But understand that this cynical inner voice is the very thing that keeps creating the opposite of what we want. So instead of truly believing that he can deliver the security we need, our deepest thought is that he never will. So no matter what we say with our mouths, that lack of trust is deeply engrained in our minds. Women raised without viable men in their lives are even more likely to have developed this lack of trust or faith in men.

This inherent lack of trust is not even the worst issue. The learned behaviors of worry and anxiety are far worse than never having learned to trust. It is terrible to worry because our thoughts remain focused on the negative possibilities, which based on the Law of Attraction, attracts negativity directly to our front doors. Worrying about our men's capabilities attracts men who cannot deliver. Remember, what we focus on expands. Then ironically, once we have attracted all that we have worried about; we turn around and blame the very men who were the results of what we had created in our minds. Due to the power of negative thinking and our inherent lack of trust, we attract negative behavior right out of even the most trustworthy of men.

Because many of us do not have a grasp on using the Law of Attraction or the concept of trusting a higher power to help us in our times of need, we use control since it is a familiar tool to us. We will take the first step of asking for what we want, but because we asked our men rather than Source itself, and due to our innate lack of trust, we then attempt to take control of the situations, or micromanage the deliverance of our dreams, which consequentially makes allowing and receiving impossible. What in the world does it mean to allow if we are in control mode? Receiving cannot happen without allowing, trusting and asking Source to deliver all we desire and deserve.

Do you see how it all breaks down on the second step because control is the opposite of trust? Control has no place in the four-step process of the Law of Attraction; it actually destroys the system. When we attempt to control, we usually end up receiving less than perfect results. In fact, we end up missing the mark completely. So let's focus more deeply for a moment on trust.

Trust implies having faith and proving it. We prove our faith when we employ positive thinking. Trust requires that we retrain our brains to believe that there is a higher power taking care of our needs. We must focus on the fact that we are protected, loved and favored by universal forces that we cannot see and may not understand, and go beyond the intellectual understanding of these forces. When we are able to trust, we can actually work The Law of Attraction in our relationships. Most of us already believe in a higher power, so why not practice trusting it. If we do not, we will forever find ourselves in situations thinking we have to 'make things happen' ourselves, or 'we have to make this man do right', or using loud and forceful words, scare tactics, withdrawal, coercion, and other nasty tools. These useless tools compromise our ability to succeed in life and love, where trust, on the other hand, ensures success.

Principle #6: Trust Source to Deliver and Your Man Will Deliver

A perpetual state of distrust accomplishes its mission by creating the very issues that we attempt to avoid. In fact, attempting to avoid something actually calls the scenario right into our lives; this is the state of most relationships. Women make reasonable requests from their men by asking for what they want like fidelity, protection and commitment. We should have asked Source instead of our men.

Then most women skip the second step, trust, and find ways to attempt to control the delivery of their requests themselves. Fear kicks in when the control tactics fail, the negative thoughts take over, and worst-case scenarios are manifested. Usually we blame the man for not following through with our request when in actuality we have thwarted our own plans with our negative thinking, fears and control. We then decide that he is simply not trustworthy and we give up on trusting men all together.

To trust a man is the single most challenging thing we can aspire to, because trusting him requires that we first learn to trust the Universe to protect us. How many people are doing that? Simply stated, a person who trusts the Universe is fearless. He or she knows that nothing can possibly happen that will not serve to further one's goals and objectives. A person, who trusts the Universe to provide all things knows that all things happen for a reason, and rarely worries, complains or loses hope.

Due to this unwavering trust or faith, these persons feel good most of the time. For them set backs are seen as set ups for MAJOR comebacks; this means that they do not let challenges or fear-inducing situations to deter them. Individuals who trust find the bounty in all experiences whether they appear to be good or bad. This opens them to allowing and then receiving bliss and to succeeding at manifesting the things they want most in life.

We learn to trust the Universe in the same way we learn to play an instrument; we must practice. I would advise that women begin practicing trust faithfully in small ways. I found that practicing to trust the Universe helped me to be able to trust my husband almost immediately. In fact, I found that practicing to trust in situations with him, was simultaneously training me to trust the Universe. My hard work paid off because in the end he became trustworthy. I did not feel as though I had to give him directions on how to go about pleasing me. I learned to trust that he would do it just right every time, and the Universe delivered big time! Allow me to give examples of the ways in which I practiced this art and how it helped me heal my relationship.

Call Me, Please

I wanted my husband to simply call me when he was going to be late coming home. In no way did I feel like this was excessive in terms of giving him a directive; this was a request with respect to basic consideration and safety. I considered it a safety hazard, being home with the children late at night not knowing where he was – and I still do. All the same, my husband does not always want to call me when he is going to be out late. He feels that if he is working late, or otherwise chooses to partake in any other activity during the evening after work, that I should trust that he is fine and will be home when he gets there. How inconsiderate! This literally drove me crazy! Everyone knows and would agree with me, I am sure, that a man is suppose to call his wife when things run late so that she will not have to worry. Well, everyone knew except my dear husband. For years we fought about this, as I persistently wanted it my way, and I would specifically direct him to adhere to my wishes. But it was hit or miss; sometimes he would and sometimes he would not. What a mess. How was I supposed to trust him if he refused to do such a simple thing? Forget about prayer, I wanted him to acknowledge that I was right and follow my dictates.

As a result of my worry, I developed a great amount of fear around losing my husband, and would have frequent thoughts of his death. As the primary breadwinner, if he were to leave us in this way, what would we do? I felt as though I could feel better if only I knew where he was at all times. Also, although I had not had any issues with him and infidelity, I felt an almost ingrained fear that maybe he was dating. After all, I was at home with babies for over ten years while he worked corporate jobs as a senior manager in a large firm. He holds a very high profile position and the ladies love him. Maybe I had a fear that he may be meeting women for drinks or moonlighting with his underlings.

Mostly, I wanted to feel assured that he cared for me. I wanted to trust him, but I set out to make him prove his trustworthiness by insisting that he call. Simply calling when he was going to be late would be a true test of his love for me. So I directed him to always call me hoping in this way I could come to know that he would never desert me or leave me in limbo. I asked and at the second step, trust, I totally missed the mark. I came to realize that at the core of the issue was the lack of trust. I did not know that I could trust the Universe to take care of me by taking care of him. Once I realized that he simply was not going to call me each and every time he was out late, I began to become deeply saddened. Not only was I pissed off at the Universe I was pissed at him! How could I ever learn to trust him if he refused to follow my directive of calling when he was to be out late?

Due to my fear, anger and dismay about this situation, the incidents grew worse. This is the nature of the Law of Attraction - that which we focus on expands. It hurt me so badly that he would not follow this simple mandate. I recall that I began thinking each day whether this day would be the day he disrespects me again by doing the same old thing. It got to the point where I could not wait for him to walk in the door late so that I could let him have it! I had set out to conquer his terrible habit by force. I had to lay down the law. The more I anticipated it, the more it happened.

I recall a day when my darling husband called me late in the evening to tell me that he was not coming home at all. He had chosen to stay in the city that night after working a long hard week to hang out with friends. They were going to the club to dance, relax and bond together. They had decided to have a few drinking games and he found himself too inebriated to drive home, and because we lived 40 miles from the city, he did not want to take a cab. He simply chose to stay at the friend's house for the evening. What?

My 'power of attraction' was working! I had focused on my fear for so long that even my 'good' man was doing and saying things that scared the hell out of me. For so long I had envisioned this day and here it was, staring me in the face. Sad to say, I used this incident as a way to give even more orders and cling to fears more tightly. When he finally arrived home the next day, I gave him the silent treatment. He had purchased a gift for me, thanking me for understanding his need to unwind. He had no idea how angry I was, after all, he had called. I informed him in a nasty voice how disappointed the children were to find him absent that morning. I even stated that I just did not know how long I would be able to live this way, thereby threatening my beloved and putting him on the defense.

It would not happen until years later when I finally learned about the Law of Attraction, that I was creating this. I finally came to the conclusion that I was overreacting mentally and allowing my negative thoughts to control the outcomes of otherwise normal situations. Duh! I could not continue imagining the worse and expecting things to change. I had to look more deeply at the mechanism creating my reality. I saw that the cores of my thoughts were wild with fear, and I would have to practice trusting that everything was all right.

My husband taught me a very important lesson that day. He told me that I was over reacting, and then set out to inform me of all he does for our family. Above my anger, he confronted me with the fact that each and every paycheck comes to me, that he gives me everything he has, pays all the bills, is here for our children, is here for me, has only few friends all of whom I know and can trust, is not the man I envision him to be, and is simply in need of a sense of freedom of movement. He helped me to understand, although at that time I accepted none of these words at face value; that he was in love with me and would always be here for me.

Why then were the words not enough? Well, because the change was not needed on his part. I was the one who needed to change my negative thinking in order for the situation to feel better for me. Whatever past situations causing my angst had to be rooted out and obliterated. I had to realize that not only was the Universe protecting me, but also this man of mine was trustworthy. He does not have to prove it; I simply needed to believe it.

Releasing the Past

So how can we release the old images that replay in our minds creating fear and anxiety in otherwise good relationships? How can we learn to trust a man to deliver all that we desire? So many or our past experiences have shown us that trusting can be dangerous, risky or harmful. I can tell you based on my experiences, that past occurrences should not be the marker for trusting in our current relationships. Difficult past scenarios usually serve to show us what we were attracting at that point. The most important way to release the past, then, is to look at the past as our own creation.

Releasing the past means ceasing the blame of our fathers, x-boyfriends and other men who have 'let us down'. It begins by seeing that the source of everything is our thoughts. What were we thinking at the times of painful past experiences? Maybe in looking back we might find the source of the pain, the lessons we needed to learn from those situations rather than the blame we placed on the individuals involved. Realizing the lessons of the very valuable past experiences we each have helps us to release the past in one clean break. I have since developed a process called Lacing that helps.

Process #7 – Lacing Exercise 1

Purpose: Enjoy this quick process in releasing the pain of the past. More information will be available about this process in my upcoming book *Lacing in Love*.

Items Needed:
- ✓ Journal
- ✓ Pen
- ✓ A few moments in the day to be alone

Exercise:

1. When in a bind of worry and fear, stop for a moment to breathe.
2. Think back to the first time you felt this way in your life.
3. Be specific, did you feel this way with dad, or with an X?
4. Once you identify the first time you felt the worry, write the scenario on paper.
5. Read the scenario a few times, include each detail of what happened at that time to cause you worry and tension.
6. Close your eyes and tell yourself that it is time to go back and learn.
7. Recall the scenario in your mind and ask yourself what the lesson was.
8. Once you get an idea of the personal lesson you were learning, jot it down.
9. Next, decide to make it right in your mind. You are going to have another chance to live it!
   - ❖ Go back to the scenario and reshape the events.
   - ❖ Fool your brain into seeing a new image, a better outcome.
   - ❖ Do this each time you feel worried about your man's trustworthiness.

This brief, yet useful practice will help you to retrain your brain. First of all, as you acquire information about the lessons you have learned in life, you practice the skill of self-reflection. Reflection in this way allows you to see that all of your experiences have been a blessing. Once you find the blessing in even the most painful experiences, you will be able to forgive those involved rather than blame them. You might actually begin to appreciate the very characters who initially caused you pain. In this way, you go way beyond forgiveness into penetrating clarity about your life.

As to why you should revision the past, your brain does not know the difference between what you imagine and what actually happened. So when you see a past event happen in a new and better way, you are programming new material into your hard-wired human thinking machine. The brain then processes this as a reality, and this new thought byte attracts similar thoughts. You will find that before you know it, your daydreams will fill with past possibilities that you had never thought of before. How fun! You will enjoy an entirely new set of expectations, intuitions and outcomes.

Enjoy the release of it all. It feeds into being able to trust – truly trust. Trust is about understanding life. By doing this exercise on releasing, you will gain a greater understanding of the story of your life. After sometime, your story will make perfect sense, and of course, you will expect that your current situations are doing nothing but weaving more fantastic data for you to learn and grow from. Recalling that trusting your man will make him trustworthy based on the Law of Attraction, this exercise becomes mandatory for the healing required for getting to the next two steps in the process, allowing and receiving. But what if your lack of trust is not something you picked up from negative life situations, but rather from a female parent who lacked trust in her man?

How to Heal a Legacy of Lacking Trust

I am now aware of the moments when I morph backwards into my lack of trusting. Relationships require trust and I truly had none. Most of us are just not from places where we learned to trust that things would be fine, especially with a man at the helm. This is not a good thing, and it does not help our relationships. Most of our mothers squawked and worried when any little thing went wrong. Most men despise following the dictates of an angry woman, and my dad was no different. He seemed so tense on a daily basis, probably thinking about when the next ball would drop. "Why are you allowing the kids to do that, they could get hurt, there could be danger," she would say as though my dad was completely clueless. What she did not realize was that he was looking at the world with different eyes than she.

Eggerichs talks about this in his very incredible book, Love and Respect. He addresses the pink glasses and the blue glasses, the varied perspectives that men and women have in viewing the world. My dad was simply looking at the world with the eyes of a man – the blue glasses. I guess my mother did not trust those 'man eyes', she felt it was pink or bust.

So as the fruit did not fall far from the tree, I came up to be similar in my distrust for a man's ability to do just about anything. I have heard the Internet jokes addressing husbands as second children and so forth, and I despise the stuff. When I married, I expected hubby to take care of me and I just assumed he would do it – my way. But as the years went by, I found myself becoming more and more like my mother, bless her heart. I began to notice that all the talk about implementing the trust that I never saw my mother exhibit would dry up when it actually came time to shut up and trust him.

I recall dozens of instances where I simply had to speak my mind and give him just one tiny set of directions. I just felt it necessary to direct this man because I did not trust that he would do it right, or quickly enough, or with enough class. I felt as though my tastes, and my ways were superior. When I directed him, I expected that he follow and do it my way. I wanted to train him into being a good man. I watched sadly as he became rebellious, just as my father had at the uttering of my mother's ceaseless instructions. Still I pressed on, giving directions and injecting control tactics, however subtly, in my relationship.

Backfire, backfire, and backfire! This stuff backfired on me over and over again in ways that I cannot even recall, and I probably have yet to connect to the passive-aggressive behavior that followed from him. I used to think that his sitting in front of the TV, or working late were probably reactions to something I had done. Little did I know that his behaviors, like other passive-aggressive tendencies, were all blockades to protect his ego from my constant giving of direction with the expectation that he follow.

Now, many of you might be thinking, "What is wrong with giving a man a few directives?" Well, the proof is in the pudding, and I had a legacy established from having watched my mother. The directives were never ending. I mean, I had a directive for the children, the groceries, the cleaning, the cooking, the proper couch to sit for watching TV, the way the painting should be done, the money, the sex, the rearing of the pets, his career, our social networking, the in-laws, the vacations…everything that we did together was subject to my spin. The message that I did not trust him was huge.

It was almost as if I was afraid to trust anything to go on uninformed by me. For example, I felt as though my world might fall apart: 1) if I left the children with him without a note on bedtimes of what to eat and how to respond to crying; or 2) I thought I would just die, and this is really true, if he did not spend that extra moment with the children reading them a story at night instead of telling them in a blunt voice to go to bed, as he preferred; and 3) then there was the thought that the house would cave in if he did not fix the disposal today, take out the trash right now, or get the socks from the floor this instant.

I was anal about little things like the amount of time he watched TV, or the content of that particular TV time. I was even paranoid about the amount of time he spent on the computer or working. I would always ask him if he could just work like a normal person with a nine to five. As an IT consultant, I know now that this would have been impossible for him.

Nevertheless, he went through a hell of a lot of years taking this from me. Truly, I guess I would have to say that I had an inability to allow and receive. I did not know how to trust him to take care of me. I could not relax into the idea that no matter how good things might appear for the moment, I felt as though I had to give directions under the guise of calling it 'helping'. I recall my Mom becoming upset at times about something my Dad was doing. She would chalk up her constant input into his doings as being a 'helpmate'. Over time, it came down to the fact that he did not marry her to be his helpmate. This is simply my observation and due to his rebellion to her 'help', one might easily conclude such. I did not want to be this way in my marriage.

To remedy this, I decided to actually use the Lacing process on myself to remove the issues of my mother, which she had probably picked up from her mother and so forth. I had to make her into a better model for me to follow. It worked quite well. I simply reworked the situations of my past in my mind making them have happier endings and gave my mom new behaviors in my imagination...

Lacing is a simple visualization exercise that has positive and lasting effects on the subconscious mind. It is actually quite fun to practice. By doing the Lacing exercises, you will allow yourself to move your practice of trusting your husband to the next level. Once you are able to trust, then you will truly be able to allow the Universe to work on your behalf, and then, oh joy, you will finally reach the point where you can receive all the bounty you desire. More importantly, you will be able to create and then receive a trustworthy man.

Process #8 – Lacing Exercise 2

Purpose: To remove the legacy of control and implant a new model for success.

Items Needed:
- ✓ A notebook
- ✓ A great instrumental CD
- ✓ Private time to meditate

Exercise:
1. Think about your trust issues. Who in your past had the same issues?
2. List the ways in which you share trust issues with a person from your past.
3. Decide that now is the time to shift this connection and recreate this role model.
4. Write out a specific situation in which this person demonstrated his/her lack of trust for another.
5. Now rewrite the situation as it could have been and how that would have been better for this person...give him/her a new response.
    - ❖ For example: If your mom had created a bad relationship ending in divorce, write down the things she said that signified to you that she no longer trusted your father. Rewrite the story on a separate sheet of paper illustrating another possibility for mom. Maybe instead of creating a bad marriage, this time she would be using the principles in this book and she succeeded in her marriage. Now she loves your father because he is so trustworthy, kind and happy.
6. Once you have your original 'bad' story and then your new possibility story, choose a time to meditate...

7. Put on your great instrumental music, breathe and relax then allow yourself to see the subject of your Lacing.
8. See the person who modeled your lack of trust.
9. See them go through the rough time again...
10. Now change the vision and tell the person that you give them a new possibility today!
11. See the person in the new possibility; the new story.
12. Feel how happy the person is now and how much they trust others!

Repeat the visions as many times as you would like to. I recommend lacing at least once a week. But this can be done in your daydreams. Giving the persons in your past a new possibility is really a gift to your spirit.

This exercise will cause your brain to actually change from the inside out. The old images and memories were creating your old reality. Now you are changing these images and memories. YES, this really works!

The brain does not know the difference between what you imagine and what you actually remember. You can change your memories at any given moment by reimagining them and making them new!

Chapter 7: Make Him Stylish – Care for Yourself

Men are so beautiful. A fine man is like a morsel of well-prepared food – delicious and totally inviting. Men of any race, size and age are even more appealing depending upon personal style choices, and enhancements that make a man just right. A man's personal style includes his clothing, his scent and choice of shoes, but can also include his vehicle, his walk and his personality. A large element of style is also his physique. Oh baby, you know the ones I mean, the well-groomed personal style, and clean-cut with a body to match! Watch out ladies, I'm heating up as I even speak the words! There is nothing more appealing to a woman than a man with a well-tailored personal style. From the initial point of contact of men with all of these elements in place, we find ourselves completely entranced by his appearance and style and we simply go gaa, gaa, and find ourselves considering ways to get him to notice us and we mean business, right ladies?

Male style and our attraction to it is actually an ancient ritual. In many ancient cultures, it was the women who chose the men. Yes, it was the reverse of today's modern courting style. Ancient women were in the position to choose and the men just sat pretty and waited for a woman to make her choice. Men would dress their delicious, cut bodies with markings and jewels and dance the alluring warrior's dance to attract a suitor in the village of women. This ceremony might happen a few times a year. During the dance and show of men, the women would come forward to choose their men. A chosen man would literally dance more vigorously even after hours of dancing to show his excitement for being chosen. Wow, do we not wish those days were back? Well, in a way this tradition still exists. Women today choose men based, first and foremost, on their sense of personal style. If anyone tries to deny this, they need a reality check.

Principle #7: Concern Yourself with Your Personal Style and Your Man Will Follow

Let's explore a common issue in relationships tied into men's style and women's enjoyment of stylish men. Because women are so moved by a man's sense of style, we expect that our man should want to please us by being clean, fresh and well dressed. Why not? It is evident that men enjoy attracting women with external expressions of their 'oh, so luscious' maleness and beauty. So why would we not expect even the worst dressed man to rise to the occasion and be stylish for us?

There is nothing wrong with the expectation. However, getting involved with a man who is a tad less than stylish happens. We ladies have a knack for seeing the potential in even the worst dressed men. When we find ourselves in a situation with such a man, it is reasonable to expect that he should begin to keep himself up to please us, right? Men do not have an issue with dressing well or looking good. They know that women appreciate a well-put-together man, as they are much smarter than we think.

The issues around style arise when we attempt to force a man into a style of dress by giving him directions. Usually when we want a man to become more stylish, even if he is already doing pretty well in that department, we decide to do one or all of a few things:

- ❖ We decide that we need to advise him on what to wear on a regular basis.
- ❖ We decide that we need to do some shopping for him.
- ❖ We feel we need to pick out his daily clothing and/or pack his bags for him.

Many women may be reading this and thinking so what is the problem? Men need our help to know what to wear on holidays and special occasions. And of course we have to shop for them they do not like the mall. Yes, we pack their bags for vacation and pick his clothing to wear to the airport, what is wrong with that? I used to believe that men do not have time or interest in this sort of thing, probably because my own father did not. It sounds logical, but for those who have tried this form of direction giving, I would be interested to know the results to date.

Personally, the times I have tried to choose my husband's clothing, pack for him, give advice on the car he needs to buy, or the cologne he needs to wear, things backfired. Instead of having a more stylish man, I ended up with a grown son depending on me to always help him with this regard. I recall the days when after lots of 'training' my husband in the style department, there might be a day when I needed him to pick his own clothes. Maybe I was to meet him at my job for an after-work gathering, and I did not get to pick his clothing out before I left. Boy, would he surprise me! He might show up in just about anything and after all the work I had done to help him know how to dress appropriately. My goodness, I began to feel that if I were not there to choose his clothing, he just would not be able to do it, and he proved this true over and over again (Law of Attraction).

Often, men begin to become dependent on women who give directions in this way. It feels good for a man at first to be babied by his woman who might shop for his underwear, manage his closet, take his shirts to the cleaners, and decide each element of his personal style. Cool, right, and very convenient for him? At first, he might feel as if he has his own personal stylist, but over time, he begins to feel smothered. Oh, I know what you are thinking. Smothered? You work yourself like a dog to manage him in this way, why would he feel smothered? Mothered is the root word in smothered and it is a clue as to why he might feel smothered under these circumstances; actually he feels mothered.

How many men do you think want to have sex with their mother? Not many that I know of. It is time for the smart women to discover something new. We naturally desire physical attraction to our mates, so it is fine to want a stylish man. Attractiveness is often associated to wearing certain clothing or driving a certain car, and especially smelling good and taking care of personal hygiene. However, when we step in to give direction to our men in this area, it takes away his precious autonomy. Do not forget that inherent in the guys who do style well, is a sense of personal dignity that has outward expression in the style he chooses.

Essentially, these well-styled men are demonstrating autonomy and confidence when they choose to care for themselves in the 'luscious' ways they do. Men want to give us their most wonderful, sexy selves, but they want to give it on their terms. They want to offer us something they have prepared and planned. They want to execute things themselves and feel successful at it. This sense of personal dignity gets squashed when we step in to dictate his personal style.

When we are the ones who have shopped for and purchased the clothing and car, instructed him on how to and when to wear the clothing, and given pointers on how to walk, talk and be the sexy man we want him to be, it robs him of the opportunity to do these things on his own and for himself, maybe even from the heart for you! He becomes like a Ken doll that is being played with by a little girl masquerading as the woman who loves him. This form of direction giving is subtle and heavily misunderstood. Women, myself included, who are guilty of it often, do not understand what the problem is.

196

This chapter lays out the inherent imbalances caused by this simple infraction and of course provides solutions. Yes, we can make our men sexy and stylish, but to do it we have to focus on our own care and fashion. If we focus on giving him directions on how to be the man we want him to be, we are more than likely to get a well-dressed little boy who will allow his personal style to diminish on purpose the moment he realizes that he is not in a relationship with a sexy woman, but instead, with another mother. I will explain further how easily this can happen…

The Moment He Notices His Mom Moved In

When I first got married at the tender age of 21, I decided that my first project would be to give my new husband a much-needed make over. I mean his style had been enough to attract me, but I had also envisions of all the upgrades I planned to download once I had him. I wanted to get him up to speed on the latest fashion trends. His body was nice and long, lean and beautiful. But he was not accustomed to dressing in the great styles that might highlight his physique and compliment his light, creamy skin.

Basically, his style and fashion sense was non-existent. Carl was in graduate school at the time we met, so I guess he did not have the money to really dress well. Nevertheless, the jeans and sweatshirt thing was not cool. The glasses needed an upgrade and his collection of shoes, which included maybe three pairs, needed an instant spruce up. He never thought to wear cologne, and his car was old and clunky; we would fix that right up. I wanted to see him be all that I imagined he could be, so I was determined to help him learn to dress a little better.

So I went about the business of changing him in a very direct way. I gave him some direction about all the things I felt

197

needed a boost. I envisioned ways I could help him be that sturdy man I saw on the inside of him. I wanted to make love to that guy! Things moved more slowly than I had hoped on that front until one day I got a brilliant idea, or so I thought. It was very close to Christmas time and there would be an opportunity to purchase gifts for him.

When my husband and I were first together, I was in undergraduate school, so money was tight. I knew that he had an American Express card and he seemed pretty much able to handle the bill each month, so I figured I would ask him to use that to go get some Christmas gifts. I failed to mention that the gifts I was buying were intended to spruce up his wardrobe. I would take his credit card and buy him a series of gifts to help him get his look in order.

On Christmas Day, we would be heading to my parents' house in Detroit to meet my family for the first time. I was determined to make sure that he looked good for my family and his. My little sister, Rashida, and I always had a running competition going with our boyfriends. I was going to win hands down this year!

So I went to the mall and on his American Express card charged a $500 leather jacket, a pair of dark brown Timberland boots to match and several preppy Gap shirts and khakis. I also picked out a new pair of glasses (something elegant and fresh) for my techie man. I could not leave the mall without purchasing a little cologne for him, something I liked, musky and rich. Happy as a fat cat, I left the mall with a twinkle in my eyes. How he would love me for this gift of newness! The praises he would sing in my honor. After all, he did not have time to shop, I did the next best thing, and I became his personal shopper. I hoped everything would fit, and he would appreciate my gesture.

When I arrived home, goods in hand, I promptly presented the bags and packages. The look in his eyes at first was excitement – this was going better than I had planned. As he tried the items on, he looked like a kid in a candy store. Sure, he did not know yet, that I had charged the items on his American Express, but he did know he liked the stuff. Looking back, maybe I exaggerate his excitement. The energy I feel today as I think on this memory is that he probably felt like a 10-year-old boy whose mother had gone shopping for him. Trying on clothing is such a drag for guys, but he did it for me anyway. He enjoyed seeing me happy, but was I the only happy one? Who cares! He was being transformed before my eyes into the stylish, sexy man that I wanted.

Soon he cracked the glee I was experiencing to ask me how I could afford such 'gifts'. Well, I told him that he had purchased all the stuff with his own money, and I had purchased it all with his American Express card. In disbelief, his reply was, "What?" He thought I was going out to purchase Christmas gifts for the families. How could I have done something so foolish? Well, at the tender age of 21 I still had lots to learn.

He asked me how I expected him to pay for all the goods. I smiled and told him that we would work it out. He was the only one working at the time, so actually I meant that he would work it out. He glared at me in disbelief. He looked at the stuff and tried to maintain his smile, pretending I guess, to appreciate me and the fact that I had actually gone shopping for him. But I could tell that he was a bit disgruntled. We were already engaged, so he could not just kick me to the curb; he would have to swallow this one. But I offered to take it all back, and of course, he said no, that he would keep the stuff. He must have loved it!

Regardless of how he felt, I was proud of myself. I was on a mission to make this man sexy and stylish. This was important to me. The only issue is that when he put the stuff on he still did not fit the bill. Oddly enough, even in the most expensive and stylish clothing, things did not quite add up. I would have to ignore this, I guess. Now I know what the issue was. A man has to have the energy of style and class, he cannot dress up in big boy clothing to make it happen. As I recall these events now, I laugh at myself. Obviously, a man who chooses his own style is going to appear most comfortable in the digs. How obscene not to have known it.

You understand the issue, don't you? It is as clear as crystal, right? Just step back from this situation for a minute, it may sound minor to do this, and let's put ourselves in his shoes. Basically, the message I was sending without saying it is that he would need me to set his bar for style. I was telling him without words that I did not trust him to do the most basic thing in the world, dress himself. I was undermining his ability to actually get into the energy of being stylish by attempting to set his standard and choosing his look.

What if a man purchased for you an entirely new wardrobe, on your credit card (if he wanted to do this with his own cash, that would be fine for me personally) without asking you, but rather telling you that you needed some new clothes and that your old ones were unacceptable for the trip to meet the parents. After purchasing these clothes, he actually showed up with the stuff expecting you to wear it leaving your old clothes that you had chosen as an adult for yourself out of the rotation. Truly, he expected you to burn the old shit and never look back. How would you take this beyond the original surprise and joy of receiving a gift? OK, this may not be the best example because women are different from men in that we generally love gifts, so to receive a new wardrobe from a man might be a welcomed surprise. But men are not women. They take great pride in making personal choices. There is nothing sexier than a man who can choose for himself and become aligned to the energy of masculine, sexy style.

Then on top of that, what if he saw you in the new clothing and his lip dropped because you were still not looking the way that he wanted you to look. Let's say you just do not possess the attitude or the demeanor that he was hoping the clothing would elicit. Imagine him wanted you to fit into his model of 'sexy', but you just did not...what would you do if you sensed it? What if he let you know it through body language and non-verbal communication, flat out with his energetic response to you in the new clothing that you still do not look good enough...

It is completely inappropriate and it is a tactic that undermines his manhood. I know I am not the only one who has done this. Please testify ladies, do not leave me hanging, can somebody testify? Amen! It is manipulative, cruel and inhumane to expect your man to meld into the image that you want for him. He was perfectly able to choose his clothing before you met, and now you are shopping for him like his mother did before his faculties were online. Why then would he turn around and be able to love you? You have shown no respect for him as a complete and whole person. Instead, you give directions and eventually it leads to downfall. There is a better way to make a man into the stylish buff that you always imagine he can be.

The Style Solution

Oh, the tingles I get on my insides when I see or smell that stylish type of men whom I love come my way. Do you get the tingles too ladies? What about the ones on their cell phones, in business suits, and stepping out of a nice SUV to match his look? Luscious! I have actually stopped to stare at stylish men on the streets lately. I have no shame in my game. I think I speak for most women when I express the fact that I want a well-dressed, stylish man by my side in life. So how do we change our men into stylish, sexy, fashion-forward hotties without directing them as a mother would? The solution is simple. Become a walking picture of style yourself and expect that everyone around you will follow suit (again, recall the Law of Attraction).

Yes, it is simple, right? Focus on your own appearance, go to the mall for yourself, and pack your own suitcase filled with all the beautiful styles that you like. Dress as though you already have a chic, stylish man. Become entranced in developing your own sense of personal style. You will not even have time to dress him when you are spending your time and money dressing yourself. How is your car, your scent and your wardrobe? Well, get into it! Spruce it up! If you do not currently have the money to purchase all that you desire, make a vision board.

Design your style based on images you find in magazines, snip the clippings that exemplify your personal style. Sure, you can include images of men's styles you like as well. Cut out all the fashions you believe you should wear and include fashion bytes for the man you love. Place your vision board in your closet. Go ahead, be corny. So what if he asks you what the deal is, tell him that you are looking to create a wonderful wardrobe, not for him, but for yourself. Tell him that these are the types of things you like. Steer clear of offering him advice, and be sure that you do not tell him that this is how you want him to dress. Allow him to simply bathe in the energy of your vision without coercion toward a given objective.

In terms of the moment, allow him to wear whatever he wants when you go out. It is worth a moment of embarrassment to allow him to see for himself the way other men are dressed when he arrives at a black tie affair in a suit, or to a cocktail party with jeans. Let him see and feel for himself how out of place he feels. Never remind him or point out to him the misplaced look he is wearing, just let him discover for himself the inequality. He can do this; yes, he can. He has to do this in order to make the mark and shift upward; he will see that for himself. Men are way more observant than we think. As well, make sure that you are dressed appropriately. Just show up classy and dreamy. Allow him to see the other men gawk. This too is a motivational factor for men. They see the attention you get and give and they want to be a part of the mix.

It takes a minute to relax into this type of training. This is a silent training ground, the best training ground for men. They want to learn by doing. Men are not into fashion advice or exploratory on proper style. It makes them feel rather young and stupid. Behave as though you trust him to take care of that for himself. If he asks you a question about what to wear to a given occasion, just tell him the basics, it is black tie or it is cocktail. Never give him specifics on what exactly he should wear. He can figure that out for himself. Giving your man fashion specifics is the fastest way to morph him into little-boy mode, which he might appreciate for the moment, but resent over time. Let him investigate things for himself. We all have access to the Internet and he can look up 'black tie'; it is not hard. Of course, we are sure to compliment him when he chooses his outfit well.

By following these simple tactics, we can make our men into super stylish men. It actually works! It has worked with my husband. Let me tell you what happened recently in our marriage. I want you to feel motivated to try this for yourself if you want your man to change right before your eyes. You can do this and so can he.

Journey of a Sun God

OK, so these days my husband is the only one who has an American Express card because he is the only one with a corporate job. I do not have access to the credit card anymore, and it is a good thing too! I am just out of control with credit cards. These days I am a cash only girl. Sure, I have a bankcard, but I have to have money in the account to spend it. I have reversed the roles back to allowing him to be the financial manager in our home, so here I stand credit cardless.

My Sun God – my dear man – was to meet me in Boston to catch a New England Patriots game. It so happens that my little brother was playing for the New England Patriots team and he got us box seats with all the other players' families. Whoopee! I was to use the opportunity to do some hot networking. My children and husband would have to look as good as I looked in order to pull off the family portrait I dreamed of, so everything had to be just right.

I had the children's look under control; they would be my Gap babies for sure with their hair and duds intact. And of course, I would look the part, fresh, elegant and classy. I wanted him to have some new clothing so that he would fit into the crowd and represent me the correct way. (Yes, even after ten years of marriage, I still fell into directing him in matters of style; I was in process, but had not yet completely let go.) So I called him from Virginia, where we lived at the time, to Atlanta where he works. I asked him to please purchase himself a coat and some outfits for the weekend. See, I was getting better, I asked him to do the purchase, and I did not go get the stuff for him. Change is good.

He procrastinated and did not do it (probably because I had weakened him over the years by going out to buy his shit for him, doing for a grown man what he should be doing for himself). For whatever reason, he did not get the job done. It came down to the weekend of the event and he was ready to fly to meet us in Boston, when he decided to go ahead and shop...last minute and raggedy.

He went to an inner-city store in Atlanta – the only store near the airport, which in my opinion, was geared to the taste and styles of inner-city youth – and proceeded to shop. This man purchased a bright white coat with the fur around the hood, you know the super-stuffed, down coats that looked like the kind an 18-year-old teenager would buy, my GOD! He also picked up two pairs of no-name jeans with the colored thread in the seams, light blue and orange. The pants were designed to sag down off the butt, and his little skinny butt definitely allowed the sag to go down with no problem. He bought two of the exact same white shirts, you know the ones that do not button, and look just as saggy as the jeans! The shirts looked like thermal underwear for winter that would be worn under a nice Polo button up; it is just that the button-up part was vastly missing. Tack-E! On top of all that, he bought some white tennis shoes and a bright white hat to match the bright white coat! Oooh my gooosh!

Now mind you, I have the three children in DC and we are flying to Boston where the sporting event was to go down. We have a separate flight from hubby who will be arriving later from Atlanta. I prepared to be pleasantly surprised by his selections, but instead, when I saw him arrive with those tacky clothes, I had a hissy fit! He looked just like some street drug dealer sitting at the corner standing out from the bums. All he was missing was a fat gold chain with lots of gaudy diamonds. Yuck! How in the world was I going to fix this? He did not fit in with the Gap look I was anticipating. Moreover, he thought he looked great! He was so proud of himself, poor thing. How in the world was I going to wake early enough to hit the malls on his behalf? The game was taking place at noon the next day.

There he was in front of my family looking like he did not have a job, or money, or family or common sense. He was looking, in my opinion, like he had just stepped out of 'Boys in the Hood' or 'Menace to Society', and I flipped. Luckily, I had been working to watch my responses to him. I was learning to be a woman – better late than never. Now, let me tell you how I flipped. I had a mental flip in my mind. See, there was a time when I would have just let him have it in full verbal assault. I would have just told him how silly he looked as a grown man, with a big corporate job, wearing 'ghetto-fabulous' gear. But that scared little girl in me was dying a slow death, and the woman was emerging. Inside I was flipping out, totally floored, but a smile dominated my face, and when he asked me how I liked his new clothing, I expressed that they were quite 'interesting'. I did not get mad and insult or confront him, I simply expressed subtle honesty being careful not to direct him or disrespect him. There was not even a hint of sarcasm in my voice.

As the weekend went on, I became more and more used to his new and authentic look. I even began to find it pretty cool that he could be this corporate big ten consulting guy by day, and this new B-boy by night. I felt kind of cool and hip knowing that he was actually being himself by wearing these cloths and that he did not always have to wear a pair of khakis to please me.

As I melded with his personal choices and accepted him for the man he was, I felt a deep sense of pleasure at seeing him so pleased with himself. I felt he actually brighten on the inside at my acceptance of him, besides he actually looked pretty cute in all that stuff. What I realized was that his spirit was coming forth; he was becoming a man in my eyes capable of making his own choices. I found that my practice in supporting him actually drew us closer. When he felt proud of himself, we became closer, more bonded. He actually became the vision of style I craved. I gained respect for him that day and I fell even more deeply in love with him for who he is, something that I had not allowed myself to do prior to that weekend because of an incessant, unnecessary need to control.

Several months later, I found myself loving that big white jacket and B-boy look. When I hit the town with him dressed as the classy diva that I am, I feel like I am on a video shot for a rap video. I could not have anticipated the good feelings that came after I released him to create himself, but it sure did do the trick. He was becoming himself and that is what makes a stylish man shine. I would cuddle up into that big white ghetto coat and love feeling my man be his own man from the inside out. The little girl in me, who wanted him to be the preppy guy that I dreamed of marrying, slowly fell away as I allowed my authentic self-birth.

Currently, summer is coming and I am reconsidering allowing him to choose his own summer clothing this year. I am tired of trying to control him in a way that seems just oh so helpful and innocent. It is not innocent and it is not helpful...he has to do him...and because he has, I have more time and energy to do me.

Try this on your own. Get into the flow of your own personal style. Birth your authentic self and allow him to do the same. I will explain the vision board process and the self-care process. Both are helpful in unraveling years of giving direction on style to a man perfectly capable of figuring this out for himself, and who must figure it out for himself in order to be authentic. If you follow this advice, I assure you he will change into that vision of style you long for. It may not come in ways that suit your personal vision of what he should become, but if you allow it, he will show you what he is made of. He is just waiting for you to let go long enough and give him ample room to find his inner style. Have fun ladies, and remember that it is good to trust, it is good to feel good, and it is good to expect the best of your man.

Process #9 – Self-Care Process/Vision Board

Purpose: To create your own personal style and place the vision into your reality so that your own mind and the Universe can make it so!

Items Needed:
- ✓ Great magazines
- ✓ One large poster board
- ✓ Scissors
- ✓ Glue
- ✓ Funky stickers or sticky notes
- ✓ A good eye

Exercise:
1. Find a spare moment when you will have about two hours for yourself.
2. Bring all of your items into one workspace to save time.
3. Look through the magazines and find the images that exemplify your personal style and the style you would want your man to exude.
4. Snip the pictures that turn you on.
5. Begin to place the pictures in a collage style on your vision board.
6. You can also write affirmations on your board where there are no pictures. Here are a few examples:
   - ❖ I am so happy that I look and feel great every day!
   - ❖ My personal style rocks. I have so many beautiful outfits!
   - ❖ I love looking good. The better I look the better I feel!
   - ❖ Oh my gosh, just look at all of my wonderful styles!
   - ❖ I am a diva!
7. Once you have completed the collage, you can begin to add stickers, glitter or other things that you love.

8. Every once in a while, you may want to document a day you looked good on a sticky note and post in on the vision board. Or you can post sticky notes when you find a great pair of shoes or outfit that you intend to purchase at some point. You might post something like this:
    ❖ I looked my very best on the cruise to Mexico! (post a picture from the cruise)
    ❖ I love my new shoes from the Gucci store. They came to me so effortlessly. (post a picture of the shoes)

♀ Change Your Man ♂

Chapter 8: Make Him Competent – Stop Competing

So now that he is as stylish as you like, let's look at the prospect of him improving confidence. You know how sexy it is being with a confident man, someone who has natural leadership skills and uses them in a diplomatic way. Who wants a bumbling fool for a man? Yet, how many women choose to think of her man as an idiot? Many, and I can attest to it. Honestly, I have found through my practice of counseling women that many of us view our men as children, or as someone we have to raise and protect. This way of thinking and not being able to find reason to see him as competent, is eroding the very essence of our relationships. We often go years with a man internally judging him, placing him in the fool's basket thinking that he will never 'man up'. What a break it would be to know that our confident guys cover everything.

Imagine waking up in the morning and knowing that the day is going to flow well. He is calm and relaxed moving through the morning without misplacing his keys, spilling juice on his shirt, or doing anything that would cause us to have to work at checking on him to make sure he has done everything right. Would it not be nice not to have to stand at the door holding the wallet that he had left on the nightstand, or remind him of meetings and inform him of after-work plans that we just know he will forget? What would the day be like if we did not have to do his tasks, balancing the checkbook, organizing the bills or any of the things that you might consider to be better off done by him. You decide on what those things are, I cannot speak for you. But as far as I am concerned, I find it wonderful to wake to a confident person, a whole human being who has his own mind, his own sense of comfort in his skin and the confidence to pull off his life without my help with everything.

Do we not just love a man who can cook himself a meal in our absence, work with the children in wonderful ways and manage the family budget? This goes way beyond taking responsibility for household chores, and it moves beyond him being a man with a sense of duty and protectiveness over the family; this is personal. It goes right along with personal style in so many ways, but it is slightly different. It goes more into the ways in which our men view us, view his position in juxtaposition to ours. Moreover, this form of confidence puts our men at the head of the family as counselor and confidant. It also informs him of his position as king in our homes. Don't you want a king? Are you willing to be a queen? Let's make our men confident. It is so easy to do.

The first steps have already been taken in previous chapters. We have put him in the position of man of the house and a responsible partner who stands up to complete his duties in the home. Now let's employ tactics that will encourage him to expand even further. Let's make him aware that he does have a voice of wisdom. Let's build into him the elements of manhood that we really want – his wisdom. Men are naturally wise; they think from the left side of the brain, the logical portion that we ladies find remiss when it comes time to deal with an emotional situation. Men navigate the world with a very even spirit, and even the ones who have not had a chance to fully develop this sense of deep inner wisdom can find it. Barack Obama has it; he seems to exude confidence and wisdom while appearing humble and diplomatic. It is in his aura and entrenched in his character. This is what we shall build next, the character and fluidity of our men's wisdom.

Principle #8: Know that Your Man is Intelligent, Wise and Powerful

Often, we feel that a man has to have knowledge in order to exude wisdom, and must be trained by modern schools, institutions and possess many degrees to get to this level of confidence. This is simply not true. Men are born with this sense of even thought, morality and honor. Women are born with natural qualities as well, but this chapter is not to expound on women's inability to possess wisdom, but rather to acknowledge the inherent dignity at the core of maleness, an insight that often goes under appreciated by women.

The main reason we fail to catch the subtle wisdom of men is that our good qualities are so all consuming. Our good qualities are awesome; we multitask and can do and focus on many things at once giving us the appearance of stealth. On the other hand, men do not multitask; they are singularly focused by nature. Because we simply do not see the bounty in being single focused, we often assume that they are less than, that they cannot keep up, and they are slow and limited in their mental ability. Again, not true. Singular focus has its benefits, and when we begin to acknowledge the inherent wisdom of their way of thinking – not to deny the utility of our own stellar functions – we begin to experience the beauty in the complimentary relationship of men and women.

Source is smart. If men and women were the exact same, we would find it difficult to really come together and accomplish things. Given the purpose-filled ways in which we were created differently, we have to recognize the difference in our cognitions as a good thing to make him confident. When we choose to see the blessings in a man's single-focused mind, we can begin to open to allowing him to use it without the infighting and competition that sometimes exists between the sexes.

We can easily make him the confident and wise person we thought we married by deciding to see the bounty of his mode of thinking. We can enhance his sense of confidence when we honor him for being and thinking exactly as he does. Here is a little story about how I changed my man from dumbo to dynamo in less than a few months. I compiled a handy six-step process from studying Dr. Laura's books, as well as The Surrendered Wife by Laura Doyle.

Dumbo to Dynamo in Six Steps

Step #1 – Stop Answering His Silly Questions. My husband used to ask me the silliest questions. I recall driving with him in the phat SUV that he purchased with a GPS system intact, a mobile phone with digital navigation in tow, as well as a fine computer and printer with easy access to Map Quest, Yahoo Maps and other great systems used for finding directions to anywhere on Earth; he is a real whiz kid, you know. Nonetheless, we would head out to a predetermined destination and he would ask me for directions. He obviously thought that with all the equipment on board that I was the handiest of them all.

I would always tell him the best ways, as well as add pointers along the way about the streets, short cuts and secret routes. I am great with this sort of thing, and I used to tease him about his warped sense of direction. A running joke was that, basically, he was going to go up and back again in circles when he chose his own route. I never failed to inform him that he was going the long way, and we would laugh about it. It was pretty funny when I told him how stupid his directions were. I would sing a little jingle that implied his stupidity. He memorized the jingle and we would sing it in unison when he found himself lost once again. Little did I know that he was singing along to the very jingle that battered his confidence?

Sure, it was fun to know that I was the better one when it came to directions, and I secretly felt a sense of superiority over him. I was actually able to learn difficult cities like Washington, DC in a wink and Atlanta in a split second, where he was not so broad in his learning curve. After almost ten years of living in DC, he still could not figure out how to navigate the city. Pity, even with GPS he did not feel confident.

One day I woke up to the sour fact that I was enabling him in his silliness. Fine, he had a bad sense of direction, but he had an excellent work ethic. He also had a great sense of technology. One day I simply decided that I was not going to insult him anymore; rather, I was going to begin to train him to be confident in his technology and sense of direction. I had thought about the reason he refused to use his onboard tools for finding his way. I realized that he would not use the GPS because he did not want to use it and fail as I sat making jingles not only about his twisted sense of direction, but also about his lack of ability even with the best navigational tools in the world. That would mean a double insult, and he just was not ready to do that; remember men are driven by success and conquest. I was not allowing him to be a success on the road. My crazy jingles and constant teasing, though done in jest for sure, were killing his sense of self. He did not like failing at that, but I kept it up and for him it was easier to laugh with me than to succumb to the fact that I was actually laughing at him.

Soon I began shifting the situations. I sampled a new technique. I started to say three magical words. Each time he asked me for directions, I used the three magical words that turn boys into wise men. Can you guess what these words are? Nooo, it is not 'I love you'. The words are even more meaningful to men than those three words. These three words work wonders in relationships where a man's assurance is in question. OK, I will let the cat out of the bag. I started to answer his request for directions with the words 'I don't know'. Yes, these are the secret words! When you say these words, men and boys have to think and act without your input. Magical! And when they do, they will see that they can do it without you. Once they know they can do anything without you, they also know they can do anything for you...

Now this takes practice, especially for those of us who are so used to providing our men with all they need. We find pleasure in helping them not to think, and instead positioning ourselves as the only thinkers. When he loses the keys and asks you where they are, just say, "I don't know." When he asks you how to cook scrambled eggs, just say, "I don't know." If he asks you the most common male question in the world, "How do you change the baby's diaper," just say, "I don't know." Your response to all things basic needs to be as such. When you start this practice, you will find that he will figure it out, and when he does, his own basic needs are met and he feels more self-assured. All you have to do is step back and watch his transformation. When he is successful at it, you are there to compliment him and tell him how smart he is; and not in a sarcastic way ladies. When he figures out what to buy his boss for Christmas and where the garage door opener is, he is becoming confident in his own abilities to live autonomously.

At first, you may feel that giving up these basics or his ceaseless need for your help, would seem self-defeating. What are you there for if not to 'help' him? Well, help is a dirty work in changing your man, and it leads to disempowering stagnation for men. A stagnant man who has no room to develop in the relationship becomes stagnant and despondent. He wants to expand himself and find his power. And guess what? He will find a relationship that will allow him this expansion, just as a rowdy teen will find expression for the experiences they crave. Try to realize that allowing him to use his own inner guidance instead of sole reliance on you will cause him to know that he is capable, free and independent. Sounds too much like child-rearing 101? Good, now you know that you are an adult. You have to accept that he is an adult too! Treating him like a child will beget a child. We want to beget men – competent and able men, right?

So over a period of time, my husband began to use those tech toys. He would look over at me and ask me what the directions were, but with my eyes closed and position relaxed, I would just say the magic words. He would seem confused for the moment, but then almost instantly he would turn on the damned GPS and get us there. I would 'wake up' when we arrived and express how smooth the trip had been, how I had enjoyed the nap and how glad I am to have him in the driver's seat. He would beam with new light. As time went on, the light grew brighter and soon he was as confident with directions as I felt I was. In fact, I found that he was actually a better driver. I told him often how safe I felt with him at the helm. I had more energy than ever before because instead of staying alert to help him during a long ride, or sing nasty jingles, I was resting my mind and my soul.

Sure, there is a learning curve here, but it does not take long. He chose bad routes at times and even drove miles on expansive highways going in the wrong direction. This was really none of my business. It gave me more time to sleep, read a magazine and paint my toenails. When he chose badly, I said nothing. I had learned to mind my business and allow him to mind his. Oh my God, what a feeling! I vowed never to enable the boy in him again; I liked this strong and wise man he was becoming. The magic words 'I don't know' had saved my life.

Step #2 – Stop Competing. I had to realize that the whole deal with the directions in the car was based on my feelings of superiority over him. Why did I feel intellectually superior to my man? I do not know. Well, that is a lie, I do know. I liked feeling superior and I loved it when he knew it. It is a habit we fall into sometimes, when he loses the keys, cannot scramble an egg or feigns helpless in dealing with the baby, and in that we find our power. We can easily do these things; how foolish is he, how needy.

Somewhere deep within I got off on these things. Oh, how cute, my man needs me. But that devilish character was hanging out on the other shoulder saying, "You are so much better than him, look at how helpless he is. Men are no better than women, stay in a position of power, and let him see how very much he needs you. You will become irreplaceable." This devil is sick in the head. The angel is non-existent. You know the one who is supposed to inform us of the inherent beauty in all beings. She is supposed to say, "Allow him to do this, he can do this, if he does it he will see his power. Allow him to realize his power. You can do that. He is your equal."

So we need to end the competition. Just nip it in the bud. Do the exercise below to find the areas where you compete and dominate. Count all the ones up you feel you have on him. Be honest with yourself. Listing them will allow you to end the antagonism that secretly arises between you and your mate at these moments. Take this important step in making your man confident. You will be glad you did.

In the following list, just place a few of the things you feel you do better than he does. It helps to open to placing yourself in his shoes. What would he say you feel you do better than him? Next to each item, place the ways that you let him know how much better you do these things. I will give you an example and then you should try to fill in the blanks. Once you do, you will know where to inject the magic words 'I don't know'.

Superiority Chart

Example:

Area of superiority:	Cooking food
How I show it	I tease him about his salty cooking, his only seasoning being salt!

Your turn...

Area of superiority:	
How I show it:	
Area of superiority:	
How I show it:	
Area of superiority:	
How I show it:	
Area of superiority:	
How I show it:	

Once you have your list, vow to move from this day forward with the magic words in mind. Be sure to use these magical words when he asks you to do one of these tasks for him. Realize that he is not asking you to do the task because he just admires you, he is deferring to you because he does not want to be diminished by your subtle banter at his deformed sense of going about these tasks. Recall that his approach may be different from yours, but warped it is not.

Once you begin to let him do it his way and honor it being done his way by allowing it to 'fly', then he will become more confident than you ever could have imagined and you can relax and do those wonderful things for yourself that you always thought you did not have time to accomplish. You will be upstairs in the bath without hearing his voice asking you something simple. You will find yourself settling into a good book as he puts the children to bed, locks the house doors, and cleans the kitchen cabinets just to display his newfound sense of acumen.

When he finally 'locates' you in the house, you will be in a good mood; good enough to tell him how happy you are that he gave you a moment to yourself. He will turn off the TV and put his new skills to work. This is what he has always wanted, to be considered confident by you. All men want to be your sexy handy man. But they lose the drive when they are ridiculed. As soon as they realize how good you think they are with everything, they flip into can do mode.

I loved the fact that I ended the competition and just let him win at life. It felt so much better to see my man win than teasing him when he failed. The sex got better, the love grew deeper, the intimacy returned and our house became a happy home. I had to bite my tongue quite often to stop the cutthroat vibration from just coming up on its own volition, but it worked! I used the duct tape on my mouth as Doyle suggests in her landmark work, The Surrendered Wife, and it also worked like a charm. (I have a feeling this form of using sparse words and more compliments and understanding works on boys too, I do it with my son and he is becoming quite the confident charmer. He will be ready for his wife and he will probably attract a woman who will allow it.) Try using less words and more silent understanding at home, and learn more magical words of praise to bring forth the confidence you crave in your man. Here comes another…

Step #3 – Say the words 'I Can't'. Ha! How many women say this on a regular basis, not many I know? This is the next step in making your man dig deep and find his own inner voice, his own inner wisdom. Similar to the magical words 'I don't know', 'I can't' serves the purpose of allowing the man to step forward in very special ways. Let me add a note of warning here, we are not going to use these words with attitude. We do not want to let our men know that we are somehow scheming them or playing games. To the contrary, we simply want to step out of their path to self-fulfillment.

It is we women who have placed ourselves in the position of superior beings, so it will only be us to correct it. As long as we stand blocking his flow of 'know how', he will be blocked. He will not stay blocked for long. He will find relationships that allow him to use his inner wisdom. Maybe he will find needy women; you know the type we look down on with sour eyes. Yup! He will find one of those types to spend his wisdom on. He wants to expand in all the ways that will allow him to feel useful and sturdy. He has to know that he has these qualities, the qualities of a real man.

It fits that when we say, "I can't," we move aside and allow him to assist us. Here is a case in point in which I would use these short, pretty words to draw out his confidence. My husband used to ask me all types of things. He would be free to cook or clean, even take care of the children as I worked at my desk writing, yet he would come in and ask me about dinner. I used to pop up, stop all that I am doing to satisfy his request. I felt this was real womanhood; I had swung the pendulum all the way south. I felt the need to satisfy his every need. So there I was, cooking a quick snack as he sat and surfed the net. Now this is a tricky situation, men do have legitimate needs for food and other nurturing. However, I had to get my husband out of the habit of lacking confidence in himself so much so that each hunger pang sent him running to me like he was my 4-year-old child. I broke the habit by injecting the 'I can't' thing.

He would run in panting about food. Were there leftovers in the fridge, snacks in the cupboard, was there any bread without mold; here he goes again. Where once I stood and stopped everything, I began to sweetly say, "Honey, I can't." Maybe I was right in the middle of something, that special paragraph that I had to complete. I would give him a time when I could help him, but at the same time leave him to his own devices in terms of getting himself settled in the moment. His response? Well, at first he seemed confused as to what to do. His tummy still barked hunger, but his usual crutch was dwindling. There was fear in my heart that maybe he would stop depending on me altogether for anything. But at the same time, I got to complete lots of paragraphs, dotting all of the I's and crossing all the T's, and it felt good.

When I would finally arrive to his aid, I would find that he had already made himself something quick without me. Wow! He could actually warm up leftovers and explore bread mold by himself! But instead of teasing him about what a nasty snack it was – pickles and grapes, yuck – I would say something sweet like, "Thanks for getting a snack, now I am going to make you something awesome. What would you really like?" This counsel actually strengthens the male/female connection. As the female in the relationship, when you use the magical words 'I can't' or 'I don't know', you are being a woman rather than a mother. These simple policies allow you to nurture him in womanly ways that go way beyond babying him, or just caring for his basic needs. He gets to see you as vulnerable, no, not as a superwoman or a super mother, but as a woman who needs her man just as much as he needs you.

When you make use of these ideas, you will find that he feels more protective of you. He will begin to realize that you have needs. No, you will not appear needy, you will just show him that as his wife, you appreciate his input and know how. He will begin finding wise ways to help and to satisfy you. He will love doing it all the more when you compliment his precision in satisfying you and himself. You will take comfort in knowing that he is confident in handling the business of the household.

What a wonderful feat you will have accomplished. Ladies, you have to try this. I promise you it will absolutely work like a charm. When done in a positive spirit of truth, you will find your man pleasing you and desiring to please you more than ever before. Things will look so different from the old days when you handled everything and found yourself weary and resentful at the end of the day.

Your sex life will improve because you will be so full of energy, which will of course, energize him to be even more devoted to you and devoted to using his smarts to impress you. Eventually, he will feel that he has what it takes to not only please you, but counsel you. He will get so cocky (in a good way) that he will see his role in the family as that of a wise leader and counselor to those who need him. What a rush for a man! The same rush you used to feel when you competed with him and won, but now in a positive and progressive expression through him. Does this not sound absolutely delightful? You have to try it!

Step #4 – Seek His Counsel and Follow it. Yes, you read that correctly. There is no need to reread it. Once you use the magical words on a regular basis, you will find yourself seeing his intelligence. You will find that his single focus is a good thing rather than a slow hindrance to all of your objectives. You will see that the way he maneuvers through life and takes care of his business peacefully and with profound grace is altogether useful. You are gonna want some of that, honey! Believe me, it is good stuff! Sexy, creamy, gorgeous wisdom will ooze from every pore of your man. Not only will you begin to find him irresistible, but you will find it hard to resist asking for his advice. You will want to go to him in times of need. You will stop calling your girlfriends for all the 'wise counsel' and you will allow him to guide you on more matters than before.

It is all a part of the process, for sure. When you find yourself with the urge, silly as it may seem, just follow it and go to him for counsel. Let him spill his beautiful mind into your throbbing heart. Oh, yes! Feels good doesn't it? Feels like heaven to go to a man, submit yourself to him in full vulnerability and honesty and ask for a suggestion on how you can live your life in a new way. Believe me men are waiting for this. They need this. Recall the needy women they seek out when they feel trapped in dead-end situations with women who will not allow the expansion of their wisdom. Now you have him just where you want him. He is feeling confident and secure and he is ready for you. He is waiting for his woman to open fully to him and believe in him so much that she just sprawls before him to seek his wisdom.

OK, I will stop with the sexual connotations, but I will never stop being an advocate of men's inherent intelligence. Yes, his wisdom can exist side by side our skillful multitasking abilities. It only takes trying it one time. Feel into yourself and ask an honest question of your man. Preface the conversation with all the ways you have seen him handle the subject matter in his own life with poise. So sweet and beautiful you are before him, respecting him, admiring him and giving yourself to him. (Ok, that is the last reference to sex, I promise.) But it is a sexy thing. It builds closeness in hidden ways and makes your relationship sane and easy. Everyone being treated as an adult lends to making an adult relationship, the one you always thought you would have.

Be sure to follow the counsel he suggested, do not go tit for tat about the actual advice by tossing in ways it could be even better or a bit different. Try implementing his counsel and then reporting back to him on how well it worked. Tell him again and again that he is wise, intelligent and powerful. Let him see you follow the advice; do not get slick. Show him that you respect him as a man and that his advice works for you. When you are seeking his counsel on a regular basis and following it, you will find that you can increase communication all around. His confidence is appealing, but it is also an opening to you expressing even deeper needs...check it out.

Step #5 – Express Your Needs and Let Him Figure Out How to Meet Them. You are using the magic words, he is treating you like a woman rather than a mother, closeness has increased and you are feeling energized. Good, now it is time to express your needs. Sure, in the past you have done that to no avail. He may have belittled your needs, or ignored your needs back then due to three simple facts: 1) you have always proven that you can handle your own needs; 2) you have always insulted him with your lack of appreciation for his feeble attempts at meeting your needs in the past; 3) He has never seen himself as a successful 'needs meter' until now; and 4) he did not have the confidence to know that he could try to meet your needs in the past. He failed too many times and had been afraid to have his ego hurt after trying again and again to please you, only to result in the same stale responses from you. But now you are 'satisfy able' and in most cases, you have shown him that you have real needs and that you trust him to counsel you on how to get general needs met. You have shown him that you will follow him because you trust his ability, and he is the fine, confident man you always dreamed of. The difference is that now you can express your needs to a confident man. He is a changed man if you have humbly followed the above suggestions.

So take the opportunity to express your needs. Do not worry about when to do this, you will find him constantly seeking you out, asking you if you are OK now that he knows you are your own person with your own problems to solve and that you see him as confident and able; so in one of those moments, open up to him. Tell him you want more free time or more dates with him. Tell him that you are feeling stuck in your position and that you want a change. Tell him you want to travel, or move, or have a new schedule. Be careful not to make a statement of exact demand. Make general sweeping statements that simply put the need out there. Forget about the time, place and details of how you want this need to materialize, let him figure out those details. Do not waste your gorgeous head in trying to control the outcome; just put the need out there. (Of course, you have already consulted Source for the answers to your problems.) Here are a few examples of this:

Correct:	I need a vacation.
Incorrect:	We never go anywhere, when will you travel with me? I want a vacation in November!
Correct:	I need a break; my schedule is just overwhelming.
Incorrect:	I am tired of doing all this work. I do see an end in sight. Can you kick in some time? How about now?
Correct:	Wouldn't it be nice to move to a larger home?

Incorrect:	This home is not big enough for us. Have you noticed? I want out of here by the end of the year!
Correct:	I want to date you again; I miss you.
Incorrect:	We never go on dates. When are you going to take me out on the town? I am tired of sitting at home every weekend.

You get the point of it, right? Make no stipulations, just a statement of need. Men love taking your needs and pondering the best way to get them handled, because they love to handle business. But you have to let them do it in their own time. Erase time and know that he will deliver. It is easy now that you see how confident he is. It feels good, so sweet in the moment. Once you put the statement out there, compliment him on some other good stuff he has done, like this:

Statement of Need:	I want a vacation.
Compliment:	I loved it when you took me to Niagara Falls, which was really relaxing.
Statement of Need:	I want a larger home.
Compliment:	This home has serves us well, I love it. I will really miss it.
Statement of Need:	I would like to date you again.
Compliment:	Remember the time we went dancing? Wasn't that fun? You swept me off my feet!
Statement of Need:	I really could use a break. I feel overwhelmed.
Compliment:	You work so hard; do you ever feel this way?

Let it rip ladies. No one said we cannot have our needs addressed. But it takes a complete man to do it. Nurture him into a position of confidence and then he will easily resolve your needs. You will be surprised at how quickly he responds, and when he does, gush it on. Mention your needs once, and only once, and then when he comes back with an idea, just gush. Even if the idea is less than perfect, gush! Once you lay on the sweetness, you might add more specifics. For instant, "You really handled that well...or...this is just what I wanted! I cannot wait until next time – let's stay even longer!"

Be sure not to become too demanding or disappointed if things do not go exactly your way. When he makes a suggestion, follow it. Often, if you try things his way for a change, you might find yourself pleasantly surprised. For example, if you wanted a date and he suddenly suggests that you join him at the sports bar on Thursday, GO! I do not care how much you hate sports. You might find that getting out of the house and trying something fun with him that he enjoys will be even more motivation for him. He will see that you are willing to have what Eggerichs calls a 'shoulder-to-shoulder friendship'. Men admire this ability that we have to be there with them as they enjoy something fun. Believe me, next time he may ask you what you want to do. Refrain from being specific even then, instead of saying, "I want to go to the Blue Room for dancing," just say, "I would like to go dancing." He will work out the when and where.

Step #6 – Be a Pal. One more thing, continue to be a pal. The relationship feels so much better these days. Now it is time to really develop adoration for your man. Approach him while he is sitting on the couch and sit close without talking through the program he is watching; sit shoulder to shoulder. Refrain from talking, and allow your man to enjoy your friendship in the way men relate. I have to point out an interesting study I found in Eggerichs book, which talks about the difference in commutation styles between men and women. It is relevant here, as essentially you are learning a new language for communicating more affectively with your newly vetted man. Now that he is taking pleasure in watching you respect and honor him as viable and intelligent, he will want to be around you more. This study should help you as you enjoy and better understand the new levels of friendship between the two of you:

> "Research studies confirm the male preference for shoulder-to-shoulder communication with little to no talking. Researchers performed a series of tests on males and females of various ages. Instructions for each pair of females and each pair of males were exactly the same: enter the room, sit down, and talk, if you wish. Every pair of females, no matter what their ages, reacted in the same way. They turned the chairs toward each other, or at least they turned toward each other, so they could be face to face, leaned forward and began talking. The males did not turn toward each other in anyway. They sat side by side, shoulder to shoulder looking straight ahead except for an occasional glance at each other." Eggeriches 2005

This experiment seems to reveal the undeniable fact that men simply are not wired to talk about how they feel. In fact, they mostly honor the side-by-side friendships, as opposed to the deeply vocal way in which girls and women relate. So in honoring this, we should begin to move forward on even keel with our confident men. This process makes a man more manly. The more manly he becomes, the more he will want you to honor that part of him. Sit near him, tone down the words and open to a real friendship. Do not worry, he too will approach you with a desire to please you and communicate in your vocal language as well. We are talking about mutual benefit here, not one-sided, doormat-style submission.

Female Power

I feel these practices in feminine mindfulness are very important. Women and men are different, yet equal. Together male and female energy make up one unified whole, and this powerful unit has the potential to accomplish greatness and bliss together! A more relevant meaning of Female Power is the power to unite with the male force and create greatness. Dr. Laura refers to it as 'Woman Power', and it is real! Using your power to transform your man will come easy to you after you absorb the real meaning of your power. Sure, you can exert power by competing with him to show him how dominant you are as a woman. Sure, Source has given us a lot; we can actually birth babies from our bodies. This is a real miracle, but without a man's seed, the human species could not continue. In fact, this metaphor is perfect to complete this chapter of making him confident.

The singularly focus of his sperm coming into the womb in one shot to find the egg is a real good analogy for his major talent. Sure, he does not have the faculties to do the multitasked labor of having monthly cycles, housing the eggs, or having a fertile uterus – a stretchy miracle that expands as a baby grows. He does not have a body with joints, muscles and tendons that actually move and allow a 10-pound being to fit inside, while at the same time feeding this being, transforming food into a substance that can sustain life, and producing the water needed to house the unborn.

We do all of this without even thinking about it. We multitask in natural ways that give a large clue into whom and what we are. We automatically apply multifaceted talents as we perform the labor of lodging the unborn. But that single-pointed, one-shot deal that he provides is the spark of life, the very element that gets our juices flowing and our body in motion to bring forth life.

Our power is awesome indeed in the most complex of ways. However, his power is pretty keen too. Strong and steady, it requires firmness, solid vigor and breathtaking steadiness for him to deliver his goods. Respecting and seeing the power in both ways of being becomes the ultimate way to harmonize in relationships. We cannot expect him to see his beneficial talents without honoring them first. In like manner, we desire he honor us. The old folks say, "You get what you give." So we choose to honor this spectacle of being that men are, and in turn, they will honor us and we will get the love we deserve and desire.

Here is a brief exercise to help you explode your female power. Find yourself completing this exercise on a regular basis, and I assure you your relationship will shift dramatically and it will not take that long. It might be ingrained and take longer for those of us who have been so used to directing our men, proving that we handle everything so well and that he is just a nincompoop. But once you dig those old weeds out of your garden, flowers will flourish, vegetables will grow again and you will find the harvest delightful and satisfying. Enjoy your man as he becomes the confident king that you expected when you started your journey. Thank him often for even the slightest shifts, and if you do not see any shifts, make some up! Use the Law of Attraction! Feel good most of the time trusting that the Universe is delivering all goodies to your front door through your single-focused, wise and intelligent other half.

Process #10 - Feminine Power In Your Home

Purpose: To create a force field in your home that will invoke the wisdom, intelligence and confidence you crave in your man.

Phase One – Purge The Old Ways

This is part one of a two-part process. You have to decide that your home is the place where the transformation of your relationship will take place. The only problem is that the old energy of your relationship is in the walls, the carpets and the plants of your home. You have to erase the old energy in order to make a clean break from the past. This exercise is the quickest way to make the energy of your home fresh.

Items Needed:
- ✓ One dozen eggs
- ✓ A free moment when no one is home
- ✓ 28 days of focus

Exercise:
1. Begin on the day of the New Moon. Look at the calendar or find the next new moon date on the Internet.
2. On the day of the New Moon, take out your 12 eggs and set your intention. Eggs are like sponges, they actually have been used to cure cows and other farm animals of negative influences. It is an old southern thing and it works well.
3. Say your prayer. Let the Universe know that you intend to cleanse your home and ask for the help of Source. Let it be known that you want to have a home in which there are two energies, one distinctly male and the other female.
4. Walk around and place the eggs in the corners of the very rooms in which you used to judge your man, control him or feel most desperate in your relationship.
5. You only have 12 eggs, so use them wisely. Place only egg in the corner of a room where mild arguments have taken place. Place many eggs in the corners of rooms

where the worst of yours and your man's temperament has been unleashed.

6. As you place each egg, continue to pray asking that the egg disperses negative energy from the old relationship.

7. Once you have placed all the eggs, forget about them. They will sponge all the negative energy from the items in that room.

8. On the next New Moon (28 days later) take the eggs up and toss them into the toilet. Do not use the eggs for cooking or toss them into a household trash bin. They must be immediately removed from your home. They are holding the negative energy that you wish to dispel. Wash your hands after you touch them.

Enjoy the purified energy; your house will feel quite light and airy!

Phase Two – Plant The Energy of Sweetness

Now that your house is nice and pure, it is time to bring in the new energy that you want present to aid you. Do Phase Two AFTER you have completed Phase One in its entirety.

Items Needed:
- ✓ A bowl of clean water
- ✓ An incense stick of sandalwood or rose (optional)
- ✓ A nice bouquet of flowers (roses are nice)
- ✓ Small amount of essential oil of sandalwood, violet or rose (can be purchased at Whole Foods or on the Internet)

Exercise:

1. Complete this exercise four days after any new moon. You do not have to do it directly after you do the eggs cleanse, but it would be nice if you feel ready to get started right away.
2. Gather all listed items to one location.
3. Choose a time to do this when no one else is in the house.
4. Take a nice shower or bath.
5. Dress in clothing that makes you feel feminine.
6. Place the flowers in a pretty vase.
7. Place the water in a nice small bowl add a few drops of the essential oil you chose.
8. Light the incense (optional)
9. Now it is time for you to go into a relaxed state of mind. Sit for while and think about all you desire in your relationship. Here is the perfect opportunity to ask Source to meet your needs and make things better in your home.

   ❖ Once you feel good and connected, stand and take the water with you.
   ❖ Start at the front door and begin walking around the house.
   ❖ Use your fingers to dip some water and as you walk, sprinkle the water.
   ❖ Affirm out loud what you want to see in the house, just ask of Source over and over for what you want.
   ❖ Pray in the language and way that you are accustomed to.
   ❖ Be sure to walk the entire area of the house – all levels and all rooms. In each room you may change your prayer.

- ❖ For Instance: In the kid's room you may want to affirm what you want the relationship to be between Dad and kids.
- ❖ Just be intuitive, you cannot do it wrong, whatever you are doing is right. You are using the water to plant your new energy all over the house!
- ❖ Affirming is simple – use statements of proclamation! Example: I am so happy that my man is nice to me! I am so happy that he is nice to the kids. I love this relationship! He treats me so well. I love this house; it is so peaceful!
- ❖ Praying in your own way is fine too – some ask, some affirm!

10. Once you have completed your beautiful prayer and sprayed your water all around the house, come back to the area with all of your listed items.
11. Sprinkle some of the scented water onto the bouquet of flowers and ask that the flowers symbolize the new beginning that you create today. Place the flowers in your bedroom or wherever you think they are needed most.
12. You may now burn a bit of sandalwood or rose incense if you prefer to. Often I take the incense around the house just as I did the water, but this is up to you. I pray out loud and talk to Source about what I want. I ask that the good forces help me in creating the life and love that I desire.

Guess what? Source always delivers!
We live in a Universe of Love!

Enjoy these processes and have a happy time witnessing the results!

Repeat the process starting at Phase One or Phase Two whenever you want to. Be intuitive! You know what is best. Recall the ancient women and their secret ways. Now you are equipped with secrets all your own. Please make them your own and watch your life shift higher than ever before! You are a powerful woman, armed with the information and the intellect to Change Your Man!

Chapter 9: The Real Conclusion – Your Man is Your Mirror

So ladies, how do we feel right about now? We have just completed the entire first volume packed full of ways to actually change our men! My next book will provide even more life-altering principles, processes and information. Yes, this is only the first volume. How exciting! Do you feel as excited as I am? Tell me the truth, what do you really think about shifting your beloved by changing your own behaviors, attitudes and ideas? Let me guess, you are probably still wondering why all the work falls on your shoulders. Why is it that he cannot do all of the freaking personal growth work prescribed here? Why is it that the 'burden' is on you to make magic happen in your relationships? When does his turn come to fix his own shit and to make everything work?

I know some of you are thinking that you were not born yesterday. I once felt the very same way. But once I got a taste of the love I was so hungry for, I did not give my sacrifice another thought. Besides, I have hundreds of clients, women in particular, that I talk to everyday and they commonly express frustration about having to change, feeling as though they are the only ones expected to do any real work healing the relationship. They beg me to talk to their husbands or mates in the same manner to make them do something to prove that they care and will cooperate. What a pity. Do you know what I tell these dear clients? It is the same thing I have to remind myself of every single day, and that is this: I create my life! I am directly responsible for the happenings of my life! I am in charge of my own happiness and I succeed by taking 100 percent authority of my own reality.

Oh, that does not sound too good either, huh? Well, what do you think your alternatives are? Do you think you could continue to live by the false notion that someone else is in control of your life, or that you can continue to play the role as a victim holding your happiness ransom, making it subject to the actions and non-actions of others? Would you continue to place your happiness on hold waiting for the day when your man just fricking gets it right, or simply wait for him to change before you felt better? Or better yet, you could literally pout like a small child until he does something nice and something fun – anything to feed your bleeding heart!

Enough! The time is now to step out of victim mode and into our real lives!
Love is waiting for us. It is never the other way around!

We do want the love that we desire, correct ladies? And we are ready, willing and able to do whatever it takes! Right? I have given you the first steps, and these are baby steps compared to book two. What you have in your hands is a manual to empower you to create the relationship of your dreams. Use it or not, you will still be held responsible for your own happiness. This is Universal Law! There is no way around it. Every religious book in the world insinuates it. Heaven and Hell are states of mind. Which do you choose? You always have a choice. It does not matter if you are single, married, separated, divorced or shacking up. The moral of the story remains crystal clear; you have to give it up to receive all you desire. Treat people the way you want to be treated... Is this not the golden rule? So why not start today?

Making Deposits into the Universal Bank of Bliss

Incorporating the principles in this book and implementing the processes is equivalent to making much needed deposits into the Universal Bank of Bliss. You do want to withdraw bliss from time to time and experience all the love that life has in store for you, right? Whoever heard of withdrawing something from a bank account without making any deposits? It is illogical. If you take the nine principles from Change Your Man Book One seriously and implement them without complaining that your mate is not doing the same, then you will have plenty to withdraw when the time comes to reap what you have sown. In this case, it is not a joint account. The bliss you withdraw is all your own!

Is it reasonable to ask why he does not have to make the same deposits? I would answer your question with this question, "Do you want the love you say you want, or are you just playing around with life?" If you are serious about life, you will note that the things you desire are entirely up to you to secure for yourself. Those who are serious about life know that making energetic deposits, i.e., your work effort and kindness, into the Universal Bank is the only way to amass a fortune.

The Universal Bank of Bliss is a great bank – the most awesome storehouse of intention in the galaxy. What you deposit there in the form of your goodness appreciates rapidly and never can be lost. Let's look at others who make deposits here every day. Whether it is hours of working to learn an instrument, training to run a marathon, or preparing for labor and delivery, the persons who want results make energetic deposits. The primary focus in the minds of very determined people is the end result; they focus on the bottom line rather than the incline.

You do not hear professional athletes complaining that they want someone else to practice for them or that no one else is going the extra mile, so why should they? You do not hear classical musicians griping that another person in the orchestra should learn the notes, that it is not fair to learn them alone. You rarely hear an intelligent mother complaining that her husband does not have to suffer the pains of labor. So why would you think it is up to someone else to make your relationship better. Who is best slated to put in the work of making it pretty and fun besides you? It is YOUR relationship. Even with what you would consider a perfect man, you would still have to work on yourself to achieve what you desire.

There is no knight in shining armor to come grab you up and release you from the pain you suffer. You are in charge of your pain, your peace and your pleasure. You secure the pleasure and indeed the peace, by taking matters into your own hands, making those deposits of love into the Universal Bank of Bliss. Athletes do it, musicians do it, and mothers tirelessly do it. Those at the top of their game all over the world do it. They do not wait for someone else to do it for them. If they did, they would never reach their bottom-line objectives and there would be nothing to withdraw from the Universal Bank when the time comes to reap.

So why not start now no matter what your man is currently focused on. Start making small deposits by shifting your focus from his flaws to your own. Then make larger deposits by being the change you want to see in him, learning the ways of womanhood and using them, and becoming mindful of the effects that you cause by virtue of your own habits and conditioned responses. Now is the time to examine this stuff! For whom and what are you waiting for? Him? OK, but you will be waiting forever…simply shameful.

I am not trying to put you down or be super harsh. I know that I withdraw daily from the Universe the bliss of my sacred and intimate union. My mission is to see to it that as many women as possible have what I have or better. The fact that there is a Universal Bank of Bliss at all should motivate you. Do you even have an account yet? Or are you one of those ladies who use cash for everything, or is living daily check-by-check, or buying things you cannot afford on credit whenever you feel you need something.

It feels so much better to have an abundance of bliss in the bank to withdraw from at anytime – no hassles, no worries. Just imagine a bankcard attached to a bank account holding millions. This is what it would feel like to have filled your life with goodness, taking the first steps toward love just because you can. This is what it feels like to be a movie star, athlete or professional musician. Don't you want it ladies? To be free from worry because you know there is always enough love in the account for you? Well then, make those deposits happily and watch your wealth of bliss expand immeasurably!

The Mirror Effect

All this talk about banks is making me want to look into the mirror. When you have tons of cash in the bank, I mean millions like Oprah; you just look better, right? Your energy is high and you feel on top of the world. Well, there is a metaphysical law that points to the notion that essentially we are energetic beings. This law says that we are literally ONE with all. That includes all humans, plants, animals and objects on Planet Earth. Because we are ONE with all – if you buy into that notion – we can affect one another's behavior. How do we do this? We vibrate. All of us naturally vibrate. We send off an energetic signal to objects and people on the planet that either attract or repel them.

Without fail, we attract others who vibrate on our level!

To make this plain and simpler, have you ever seen any bums living in the midst of the super rich? Well of course not! I do not mean sleeping outdoors, I mean living in a house on the same block as let's say, John Carey? You will never see it!

A bum is not vibrating at the same level as a John Carey (who was once a bum on the street I might add, but changed his vibration by carrying a fake one million dollar bill and using a couple of basic affirmations). Bums live how and where they live with others on like vibrations. The super rich live with their counterparts on like vibrations. Oooh, it is fair honey! The government did not cause it. The Law of Attraction makes it so! My point? We are always attracting who and what we are. Point blank and period...

I am writing this section to silence the fears of those who might believe that making deposits of love will never be enough to change your man. I dare say that you are with whom you are with because you are vibrating on his level. Oh shoot – I must be tripping, huh? You are not vibrating like that disgusting man. No way. Here is a little newsflash for you – YES YOU ARE! Whatever he is doing that disturbs you, is the very thing that you do not want to see about yourself. That is why you might be in denial for the moment. But once you wake from your tryst know this, he is you. He has you down pat!

This African proverb says it best: You can never see your own backside, it takes others to show you what needs cleaning and what looks fresh. This quote has nothing to do with the anal cavity. This proverb is pointing out the very energetic principle I am explaining to you. Your human counterparts are those in your space; the ones you have attracted out of the 6,853,842,282 plus human beings on the Planet Earth. You could have been born anywhere to anyone. What are the odds that you would have those parents, those children, and this man? Slim I tell you, very slim.

You choose them with your vibration. This is how magic is made! You vibrate and they come, all of like mind and spirit, they come. What a great thing! The proverb begins by stating that we cannot see our own backsides, simply put it means that the people you attract are the only ones who can show you who are – even the parts of yourself that you can't readily see. How do they do this? Do they write a term paper on it or send an email to clue you in? Hell no! They mirror you.

Yes! They show you your glorious reflection, the good the bad and the ugly. And they are not like regular mirrors; they are more parallel to those aggravating mirrors that show you your reflection 1000x! You can see every blemish, every wrinkle and age mark. The wisdom of the ancient ones is incredible. They said that you can never see your own backside without others to show you. And it is all so true. You cannot possibly know where you vibrate until you look at your life, your boss, your children, your parents and infinitely most importantly, your man!

So how do you look? Do you like what you see? Now, here is a clue as to why and how you ended up with this book in hand. You see, most of us are taught that someone else is screwing up and that we are, of course, perfect. But the ancients, in their bountiful wisdom, knew this is not so. So is this mumbo jumbo still relevant and can we apply it to our current life situations, or should we stick to a rotting paradigm that has proven time and time again that it does not take into account even the most basic Universal Laws? Yes, I am talking about the modern relationship situation. It is incomplete because it does not allow truth to be told. We are mirrors of one another and no one tells us this until we have suffered numerous serious blows in life and love. Well here I am, allowing you to discover through my stories that your love life makes perfect sense.

He is you. You are he. We are all ONE. We attract our vibratory match, nothing more, nothing less. So how does that help those who are still fearful of being the first to change, maybe the one partner taking full responsibility for the relationship? Moreover, how does this help the masses, men and women alike, who blame, shame and ridicule their very own beloveds for not being as perfect as they are? And how does it – can it – motivate you to take action making love deposits to change your man to boot?

Simply put, we are all making our beds; I am speaking literally here. You know the ones we have to lie in night after night; where pleasure is either absent, present or somewhere in between. By behaving in the ways we choose, we either make that bed cozy and comfortable or disgustingly uncomfortable. It happens folks. I saw the Oprah show about bed bugs...naughty critters they are climbing into our orifices at night, eating the rotten flesh and human discards on unwashed sheets. How long would you allow your bed to collect mites? Would it not help to recognize that you have a choice to either make the bed with fresh linens or leave it for the bugs? Your bed is made of your choices. If you alone make good choices, you sleep fresh and undisturbed by the night crawlers. So no matter what your mate feels like doing, you always have the option of making that bed fresh daily. After all, you sleep there too. Why would you wait for him while sleeping on bugs in the duration?

This analogy doesn't end with who makes up the bed. If your relationship is synonymous to a bed and you are waiting on someone else, like your man, to come and make it up for you, then I really feel for you. It is only when you wait for someone else to come make up your bed that you get into deep water. The only other option is to hire help! Who am I to tell you not to hire help, just like Oprah? But guess what you will need to do that – you got it – cash in the Universal Bank of Bliss! Do you have extra to hire help? The help of Universal forces like 'good karma' are always helpful.

Funny how we circle back to the beginning time and time again, and the only journey we have taken is within. Is it a good place, within? I sure hope so because you will attract who you are. But for those sick of metaphors, I will be clear. Here is your real protection from the harm you irrationally think will come to you if you make the first move to make your relationship work. As soon as you decide to work some of the principles expressed in this book, your man will immediately be affected, and will have to make a choice.

If he is to remain in your bed, he will have to become an energetic match to you. You will never end up with a bum in your bed if you are not a bum. If he is not, will not, or cannot become that perfect match to your new vibration, he will fall away from you and immediately be replaced by another who is. It will not feel painful and it will not be forced. Just know that you are changing for your own good!

It is not really a sacrifice, as you are raising the level of your own vibration so that you can attract a better relationship with him or someone far better. If it is humanly possible for him to rise to the occasion (and I believe that all things are possible), he will remain in your life. If he cannot, he will have no choice but to vanish from your life, and easily and swiftly be replaced by a partner worthy of the new you.

What is that? Oh, more fear. I hear you ladies. You do not want him to disappear from your life. You want this man and only this man. You just want him to straighten up and fly right. Well, I do not think this is true. If you wanted this man, you never would have picked up THIS book. You would have tolerance for all his quirks and accept him, flaws and all, and you would never be reading up on how to change him. Let's be real, you want the perfect relationship. You do not truly want this man. You think you want him and you feel you have a strong desire for him because the larger parts of you know that he is your perfect mirror and that if you can change him, you will know that you have also changed from the inside out. This is a quest that will never stop as long as humans walk the

Earth. It is called the process of evolution. We are bound to it and so we have to love it.

You attracted that man to you for a reason, and even without conscious knowledge of it, you chose him for a purpose that he has to fulfill. But what if he cannot? What if there comes a point when you do evolve away from him? Let me put it more plainly. As you evolve, he too will be forced to change or vanish. But you do not know who you will become, none of us do. Our higher selves know, but as for the 10 percent of us that we call consciousness, we are clueless.

How do you know that when you reach that elevated level that you will want someone (assuming it were possible for you to have someone who does not vibrate as you do) who is not your soul match? As I said before, you may think you want this man because currently you are vibrating at his level, however, the moment you decided that you wanted more love and affection, as well as more time, intimacy, and commitment, you found this book! And if you practice the information not intellectually, but practically, you will raise your vibration. As you do, you will watch your man transform before your very eyes. But as you become new, you may surpass him and if you do, you cannot be afraid of the bounty the Universe has in store for you. How could you possibly be afraid of something better?

Life is dynamic. Everything must change. You are going to begin making consistent deposits of love into your bliss account and making withdrawals so often you will forget the work it took to accrue your fortune. At that point, you will be able to receive love so freely that you will attract not only your man closer to you, but all men matching your vibrations will be peeping you out! You will become one of those women who exude femininity, character, warmth and radiance. You know the type who seems so happy all of the time, so rich with essence? You will become one of those sophisticated man magnets and you will love it!

And a final point to those who still fear a shift upwards, as silly as it may sound, your man is probably prewired to evolve at your pace. After all, if your man is your mirror, then he is also mirroring your desire to change and grow. Somewhere in him is the same core you exhibited by reading this book. You want to make your life better, and you are willing to work for it. As you look into your mirror of a man, you will see that reflected right back – a real desire to change. (That is, if your desire to change is sincere)

A Special Not To Single, Married, Divorced and Relating Women

Single ladies - hats off to you! You now have a model of functioning that will get you further in love than ever before. We want it all, right ladies? And we can have it all. If you begin to incorporate the principles of this book into your dating, you will find an easy path to the relationship of your dreams. This is the information that mama never told you. If you were fortunate to have a mother who knew the secrets to womanhood, she would have mentioned the very same principles that you have read about here. Put them to work and never forget that you attract who and what you are. The more you dive into ultra feminine mode, the more men you will meet who are in ultra masculine mode, and boy, are those some fine, sexy men!

Married women, I do not believe in divorce because it is a force. The name of the game is energy flow. If you are working to lift your vibe, then the Universe has your back. Even if you are not working on any front at anything, the Universe is still supporting you. By this I mean that you will always and no matter what attract who and what you are. Thus, if you attempt to force a divorce because you are just not happy, then you will end up in another relationship with another man who pushes the same buttons that made you 'just not happy'.

You cannot run away from your own vibe. Have you ever seen Charlie Brown and the little friend of his who has dust always hovering around his body? Did you want him to run as fast as he could to leave the dust behind? But no matter where he tread, that same cloud of dust surrounded him like an aura. That is just it, the behaviors you hate, the old habits and played out patterns are all your aura. You can go here or there, you can go anywhere, but that cloud of your own making is always there to greet you.

Do not fool yourself into believing that this man is doing something to you to make you unhappy that a good man just would not do. You will forever be on a treadmill of disgust with your life. This is not evolution, this is stagnation and it leads to the death of the soul. You too can use the processes in this book to develop your own inner self or to evolve yourself out of the marriage. But you cannot do it with that intent. Your intent has to be functioning the best way you can by making the deposits, changing the bed sheets and transforming yourself. Loving him is mandatory. And if you are sick of him, just look into the mirror to remember who it is you are really sick of. You have always had the power to transform your relationship and now here is your chance. Once I heard Dr. Phil say that you have to earn your way out of a relationship, and I wholeheartedly agree. I would only caution that your intention is key. You want to do this work with the intention of healing your existing relationship and wait for the Universe to do the rest. Be sincere and open to receive love. If it can come from your current mate all juicy, sweet and nice just the way you like it, you are telling me you would refuse? Nonsense.

Divorced women, do not get all nostalgic on me. I know as you read that last paragraph you went strolling down memory lane thinking about what could have been if only you had known then what you now know. Alas, here you are seeing the truth of the matter. I am sure you have experienced it now that you are out there on the dating scene, involved with another man or two or married to another man, even. It is the same old stuff ain't it? You may have noticed you are still attracting men who cannot commit, are adulterous, and are afraid of intimacy and so forth. The only divorced women who would disagree with me on this point are the ones who did the work. Now they are all shouting, "I did the work, I am exempt from your wrath Kenya K!" But you will find my estimation is true, that more than half of the divorced women in the United States are still not happy, even in their new relationships.

Why is that? It goes back to the simple fact that we are energy, pure and simple and we attract energy of like vibration. Commonly I was asked prior to releasing this book if Change Your Man is a cute way to say 'switch your man', check him in for another one. You get that, right? I would marvel at the curiously vast number of women creaming to buy a book about literally changing out their men, trading them in for an upgrade. This is not like a cell phone store! Your man is not a late model iPhone; you cannot change him out! All you can do is upgrade your vibration to attract better.

So divorced ladies, alas, all is not lost. You can begin today. If you did not do the work of changing your X-man while you were in the relationship by making viable deposits, now is your chance. Believe me the Universe gives us eons of chances. That bank account was a trust we inherited at birth. I am sure that by now you are in the same trap you found yourself in during your marriage. So use one of those new guys to practice these new skills and watch yourself rise!

Relating women, do you know why I call you that? Well, it is because you have never been married, you are not single, and you have a long-term relationship or either a series of short-term relationships. The most exotic of you have many relationships happening all at once. Oh no, I am not player hating, I just calls it like I sees it. (lol) Do not hate the player, hate the game, right? My only unsolicited advice to you is that you use the principles in all of your interactions, and on men in general. As you do, you will see how easy it is to get what you desire from your harem. Ha! I am not one to push marriage and family down people's throats. If you prefer the single life, so be it! Have fun, but play it safe by shoring up your Universal Bliss Accounts as well. It will pay off in the long run as you move up rungs of the vibratory ladder attracting higher quality guys as you go.

This information is useful for traditional and non-traditional couples. Men dating men, women dating women and poly groups. There are still lessons to be learned, you have not escaped the world of energy. You are indeed ONE with all the rest of us normal, boring folks. You will be expected to see the mirror in your partner no matter where you go. And it is only when you refuse to see the parallels between you and your beloved that you will wake up unhappy. Blaming, shaming and ridiculing someone else for the bed you made will not get the bed bugs out of your hair. Those creepy creeps are only destroyed with the work of changing those sheets, changing your habits expectations and behaviors. You know that you are loved because it is free to open an account. Love is just right there waiting for you to recognize.

The Real Bottom Line

For too long we have ignored our power to transform the very fabric of our lives. Let's reeducate ourselves in the ways of wisdom. We choose heaven or hell; they are states of mind. This is my humble perspective. Changing my man worked for me and healed the cancer in my womb. What illness can a shift in focus change for you? You are here on Earth to succeed at life and love. You can have, do or become whatever you desire. If real, lasting, powerful, fulfilling love is your desire then let's make it happen ladies.

Armed with new information we must always:

- ☛ Make our beds and lay comfortably in them...
- ☛ Make Bliss Bank deposits, amass a fortune in love!
- ☛ Be our best selves so that we can attract the best from others!

More practically:

- ✱ Implement the nine principles from Change Your Man.
- ✱ Enjoy the innovative processes from Change your Man.
- ✱ Make a womanly shift for the good to Change Your Man.

Finally:

- ♥ Love Yourself.
- ♥ Love your Man.

For goodness sake...
Who else reveals to you your very own backside?
(Try to see it on your own – I mean without a mirror!)

Change Your Man Principles – Short Glance

Principle #1
Release Your Man from Your Opinions

Principle #2
Use Your Intuition To Determine Your
Gender Role

Principle #3
Be Pleased By Every Intimate Action Your
Man Initiates

Principle #4
Appreciate Your Man's Ability To Create
His Comfort

Principle #5
Treat Your Man Like An Absolute King In
Public and in Private

Principle #6
Trust Source To Deliver And Your Man Will
Deliver

Principle #7
Create Your Own Fabulous Style And
Your Man Will Follow

Principle #8
Know That Your Man Is Intelligent, Wise And Powerful

Principle #9
Believe That Your Man Is Your Mirror

Receive Great Coaching on CYM Principles Here:

If you are interested in getting one-on-one coaching on the principles of Changing Your Man, simply visit our website.

www.jujumama.com

Here you will find personal life coaching and relationship services that suit the needs of your circumstances and budget. It's easy to change when you have support of knowledgeable consultants who understand the process.

Go to the link above and see the myriad of testimonials from women just like you who have changed their relationships for the good by employing the principles given in the chapters of this book.
Want more personal stories from the desk of Kenya K Stevens?
Go to my blog:

http://jujumama.wordpress.com

For local study groups and support circles, see either the blog or website. Find friends who understand your life.

Get inspired to Change Your Man today!

Look for Change Your Man Book 2 coming soon...

Index of Minor Processes

About the Author

Kenya K. Stevens received her BA from Howard University in Washington DC. She is founder and co-founder of three innovative companies, JujuMama LLC, SunraZe Coaching LLC and Self-As-Source Publishing LLC. Author of three popular Internet Blog sites, Kenya K. shares her formal training and experience using metaphysical principles, like the Law of Attraction, to produce practical results for her chic clientele. She is a motivational speaker and premier life coach. Kenya K. is the host of three Internet radio shows recorded live, weekly via www.meetup.com. She has her own Internet Podcasting Channel – Juju's Love Pod.

Change Your Man is her first full - length publication. She has already written book two of the series. Kenya K. is a proud cancer Survivor and aids women nationwide in reclaiming the sense of womanhood that, in her opinion, is the cure to all female reproductive illness. In her free time she enjoys meditation, yoga and metaphysical studies. Kenya K. married in 1995, at the tender age of 21, to Carl Stevens who she met on a blind date while attending Howard University. They have three, wonderful children together, Senbi Ankh, Sanu Saa and Kaheri Shemsa.

Made in the USA
Lexington, KY
19 January 2014